How To Get Rich Quickly

Proven formulas and dirty tricks of retired businessman

Andrew Preshovus
Copyright © Andrew Preshovus
All rights reserved.
Second edition: 2014

This book is dedicated to all men and women who risk every day their money, time and career in their businesses, while helping others and keeping the spirit of morale business making high.

Legal note: Copyright © 2014 Andrew Preshovus, www.preshovus.com. All rights reserved.
No part of this publication shall be reproduced, transmitted, or sold in whole or in part in any form, without the prior written consent of the author. Users of this guide are advised to do their own due diligence when it comes to making business decisions and all information, products, services that have been provided should be independently verified by your own qualified professionals. By reading this guide, you agree that I am not responsible for the success or failure of your business decisions relating to any information presented in this guide. The information contained in this guide is for informational purposes only.
I am not a lawyer or an accountant. Any legal or financial advice that I give is my opinion based on my own experience. You should always seek the advice of a professional before acting on something that I have published or recommended.

Contents

INTRODUCTION 1
MYTHS AND TRUTH ABOUT MONEY AND SUCCESSFUL PEOPLE 4
    SHORTCUTS TO BECOMING WEALTHY – HOW BRIBING WORKS 9
    HAVING MONEY IS IMPORTANT 15
    WAYS TO GET RICH EVEN QUICKER 16
    HOW TO GROW MONEY 20
    HAVING MUCH MONEY IS BAD FOR YOUR HEALTH AND HAPPINESS 22
    HARD WORK AND DISCIPLINE VS. LUCK AND FUN AT WORK 24
    WHO IS MORE SUCCESSFUL IN BUSINESS? HONEST PEOPLE VS. LIARS, BRIBERS, MANIPULATORS 28
    SYSTEMATIC PLANNING VS. INTUITION AND AD HOC PROBLEM SOLVING 31
    YOU NEED TALENT AND CHARISMA TO BECOME WEALTHY 34
    YOU NEED MONEY TO BECOME WEALTHY 36
    HAVING THE BEST PRODUCT OR SERVICE IS THE MOST IMPORTANT THING FOR HAVING SUCCESSFUL BUSINESS 37
    I AM A LOSER, I WILL NEVER BE WEALTHY 39
    THE CUSTOMER IS ALWAYS RIGHT 46
    MONEY WILL CHANGE YOUR CHARACTER AND YOU WILL BECOME A BAD PERSON 48
    YOU CAN BECOME WEALTHY ONLY BY LOOKING WEALTHY 51
    I AM TOO OLD TO BECOME WEALTHY 52
    FIRST YOU HAVE TO SAVE MONEY 53
    LIVE BELOW YOUR MEANS AND BE FRUGAL 54
    YOU HAVE TO KEEP YOURSELF AND YOUR FINANCES UNDER CONTROL 58
    DON'T RENT, BUY 59
    I DON'T NEED TO WRITE DOWN PLAN, I HAVE IT IN MY HEAD 61
    TIME IS MONEY 62
    YOU HAVE TO BE INNOVATIVE AND CREATIVE TO BECOME WEALTHY 65
    SPENDING TIME WITH YOUR BOSS CAN INCREASE YOUR SALARY MORE THAN EXCELLENT PERFORMANCE 68

BASIC TYPES OF RICH PEOPLE 72
    LOTTERY WINNER 72
    INHERITED WEALTH 74
    MARRY A MILLIONAIRE 76
    ILLEGAL OR IMMORAL WAYS TO GET MONEY – THE QUICKEST WAY 77
    GET A HIGH PAYING JOB 79
    BUSINESS OWNER 81

Training rejection by dating women 87
INVESTOR/TRADER 93
REAL ESTATE INVESTOR 96
INTELLECTUAL PROPERTY OWNER 98
PAPER ASSETS OWNER 99

KNOW YOURSELF 101

PRINCIPLE OF HAPPINESS AND THE MEANING OF YOUR LIFE 104
WHO AM I? 106
YOU CAN ACHIEVE ANYTHING YOU CAN IMAGINE - ONCE YOU WILL DEDICATE YOUR LIFE TO IT 118
YOUR MOTIVATION, SUCCESS AND FAILURES 122
WISH FOR MORE PROBLEMS TO SOLVE AND WISH FOR MORE SKILLS 124
YOUR MINDSET 127
YOUR HABITS 133
STRONG WILL, HARD WORK 135
TIME MANAGEMENT, WASTING TIME AND FOCUSING ON PRIORITIES 142
   Example of daily schedule 143
MONEY, DEBT AND RISKS 146
ACCOUNTING, NUMBERS AND ANALYZING ASSETS 150
MENTORS AND ROLE MODELS 156
THE RICH YOU 158

STUDYING IS NOT ENOUGH! 161

LEARN TO HANDLE YOUR FAILURES AND SUCCESSES 164
   You will make mistakes and that's alright 166
   When something bad happens to you, look closer, it can be a hidden blessing 167
   Forex disaster 171
   You have to stay calm during the catastrophe 174
   High performance and relax 175

HOW TO SPEND YOUR MONEY 178

   Cash flow control 183
   Assets and investing 186
   Types of assets 189
   Investing 192

WAYS TO GET RICH 196

BUSINESS OWNER 198
   Market, marketing and SALES 201

 How to handle objections - theory..209
 How to handle objections – what really works.......................210
 Art of negotiation – learn how to say yes and no....................212
 With whom to do and not to do business................................213
 On breaking promises..216
 Managing people...216
 Hiring and keeping the right people.......................................220
 25 free tips on hiring and managing people...........................226
 Example of operation manual for sales manager (SM)...........230
 Advices on leadership..234
 Six tips that will get you started..241
REAL ESTATE OWNER..243
 Real estate investing check list..246
 Rules for managing R/E property..248
PAPER ASSETS OWNER..250
INTELLECTUAL PROPERTY OWNER..252
WHERE CAN YOU LEARN AND GET EXPERIENCE..254
 Study books, read articles...254
 Mentor/coach..254
 Seminars/classes...255
 Learning by becoming an employee.......................................257
 In your own business...258
 By investing experience...259

SIX STEPS THAT WILL MAKE YOU SUCCESSFUL...................................**261**
 1. Do you really, really want it?...262
 2. Goals setting..264
 3. Action plan...266
 4. Disciplined action...270
 5. Study..272
 6. Review your plans periodically...272

BONUS CHAPTERS..**274**
 OWNING VS. CONTROLLING..274
 YOU WILL GET WHAT YOU FOCUS ON AND WHAT YOU EXPECT TO GET.............277
 WARNING! BRAIN PROGRAMMING AND POSITIVE THINKING.......................279
 LEARN TO PROGRAM YOUR MIND...281
 HOW TO VISUALIZE..283
 HOW TO FOCUS...283
 27 RECOMMENDED READING / LISTENING / WATCHING SOURCES..............285

Introduction

So you are a get rich quick wannabe, right? Welcome and find out which ways you read/heard about really lead to riches and which are just distractions losing your time.

How do we know if a man is a rich man? If you are able to control more money than other people around you, you are considered a richer and more successful person. You will be looked upon as the person who did it. It is not necessary to have billions of dollars or euros. For financial success it is necessary to have enough money to cover all your costs and live a financially worry free life. In order to have the SOCIAL status of financial success, you need to have more money than people you compare yourself with in the society. If they have one million, you want to have one million and a half. If they have one hundred thousand, you want to have two hundred thousand etc. There is a difference between being financially free and between being recognized by the society as financially successful person. So a rich man is not about having certain amount of money, but about having more than others around you.

An example can be pharaoh of Egypt thousands of years ago. He had no TV, no air conditioning, no foam mattress bed, no cell phone, no computer and even no internet. Can you believe it? ☺ But he was extremely rich and powerful compared to other people of Egypt. So if you want to be rich, you have to have much more compared to other people around you. In thirty years maybe everyone will earn few millions of dollars in his day job. It is not about how much you have, but how much you have compared to what others have.

In this book I will share my knowledge about how to get financially free. This book is not only a collection of experience which I was able to get myself but also a refined summary of all the books and articles I read over the course of ten years. As I spent four years teaching at the university while I kept my day job and started and sold two businesses, I could test what were financial myths and what really worked. And I have to tell you, some of advices I took made me lose a lot of money. It is painful to see you were conned or made some stupid investments like invest in gold and silver and then watch how its value drops. Or to sell your company and receive only partial payment with having to go to claim enforcers and the court to get your money. But do not worry, I have made the mistakes for you and I will lead you through the get rich process with less pain avoiding many mistakes beginners have.

I will show you the myths I believed in before and which I had to let go as I tested them against a real environment. This book contains short stories that represent many real life examples of success and failure. You don't have to be smart to become rich. All you need is to be bold enough to take action and know how to use people to your advantage. Social skills are more important than your intelligence.

In this book we will also cover the most common ways to become a self-made wealthy person. There are many ways to become rich, but I would not recommend some of them. They may work, but I have not enough experience with them to give you advice. And let us skip the ways of politicians, bankers or marriage in this book. They work, but you have to lower your moral standards quite a lot if you want to use them on your way to riches.

There are various ways to become wealthy and the "right way" is dependent on you. Getting wealthy is not meant for everybody. Getting wealthy is a process which can take even few decades and it can ruin your relationships. We will shortly describe ways how to get rich quickly, but these ways are not always something I recommend you to do. I will just give you options which lead to riches, but it is YOU who has to find his limits of what makes you sleep soundly during the night and which actions are behind the line of your moral compass. Let's get started!

Myths and truth about money and successful people

I have read many books on what kind of person you have to become to become wealthy. Mostly they shared advice about being an honest and disciplined person with integrity. I agree that this is how it should be. However when I see wealthy people around, I know this is usually far from the truth. Most of quickly made millionaires grew their wealth so fast because they used their opportunity to bribe government personnel or top managers in large companies. Best option for a young wannabe millionaire is to have an uncle in the top management of a bank and sell some IT system to the bank for millions. A software and IT company with the right networking is the easiest way to become rich by doing own business. Let's have an example.

One of very famous software company was started by the team of IT specialists leaving their jobs at Company A and creating their own Company B. They were the only ones who understood all the complicated systems in Company A. Company A is a huge state monopoly with high profits. What the IT guys did was to offer their services to Company A for a really high price. As they were the only ones who understood the systems, because they created it, they got the contract. I don't blame them, as my first company started also with a not so fair advantage. From what I heard, this process is normal and healthy for the market. You are employed and work for someone until you realize that you can do the work better and then you start your own company. I know of at least three other people who independently did the same with the company I worked for. We were sick of the company's system and wanted to create something better. I wanted to create a better workplace for my colleagues.

We would like to believe that only hardworking and moral people would become wealthy, but the facts say otherwise. You can be a lazy, ineffective liar and still become wealthy. You can be alcoholic and still become wealthy. It is like the difference I saw when I was teaching students at university and when I was running my business at the same time. In many schools students are taught how it should be, but in reality they get experience on how it really is. That is why experience matters more than academic education for most jobs.

Becoming wealthy has nothing to do with morality, even if most of the authors are telling us it has. Money and wealth do not discriminate against people. You can be a good person and become wealthy the same way as you can be bad person and still become wealthy. I saw many times that someone who considered himself a "good person" had no problem breaking his promises get ahead faster than people who valued their words. I don't like it, but I see it all the time. Liars do lie and when you stop doing business with them, they find someone else to cheat. There is no liar who will agree that he is a liar. It is not good for their self-image and most of them can't admit that they are liars even when caught lying. They always have their own version of the truth and there is always someone else to blame. We don't have to like it, but their approach makes them rich faster.

I am here not to judge you but to help you to become successful and wealthy. You can replace word liar with *good manipulator* or *smart* guy or *experienced* guy if it suits you. Other popular term I heard from liar when she was talking about herself was that *she just has very good social skills and emotional quotient.*

If you are interested in personal development, first you should understand yourself and start building your future based on what you are good at. Don't try to completely change yourself. It is waste of energy and time to focus on what you are bad at. Focus on your strengths and be aware of your weaknesses. Do what you are good at and let someone else do the things you can't. If you are a good manipulator, socialize easily etc., use those skills legally and morally and you can become wealthy faster. If you are a good planner, analyst etc., use your skills. Even alcoholics and drug addicts can become wealthy if they find enough courage to create assets. And they often do because they have nothing to lose!

It is said that 86% of all millionaires are self-made millionaires. There is nothing you can do about whom you were born to, but there is everything you can do about whom you will become. Of course you can try to be adopted by the millionaires, but that is similar to marriage to a wealthy partner. It can bring you money, but you will not find out and experience how to make wealth, only how to use it. To keep wealth, you have to understand it and experience creating it on your own. Having someone who loves you to pay for your spending without giving him the same value back, looks to me like behavior of a not fully grown adult. But there are exceptions of course. There always are exceptions. Exceptions, exceptions, what we would do without them? An exception for being able to take care of themselves are the pregnant women – they simply need our help during pregnancy and when raising children – it is natural. For thousands of years males were there to protect the family members and provide the family with shelter and food and women were there to give birth to children and to prepare the food. Even today (but they were taught not to admit it openly) women expect the real males to provide the family financially for the shelter, food and protection. It is hard for a woman to be good wife and mother if she has to work all day and fight like males. This is the reason why the richest guys get the prettiest girls. They radiate alpha male charisma around them and women are attracted to this radiation if the guy does not behave like a jerk.

Becoming wealthy is **simple**, but **not easy**. You can get very rich just by following e.g. this simple formula – buy low, sell high. Find where you can buy the item for low price and where to sell it for high price. Then go buy it and sell it. Sell it and then buy it is even better timing. Then repeat the process until you get rich. Stick to this formula and avoid any distractions.

There will be obstacles you will have to cross and to cross them, you will need motivation. The most common motivation is the desire for power, for women or for beautiful things you wish to possess. But it can be also be revenge, the necessity to prove to someone how capable you are, or the fear of losing financial stability, a luxurious life or losing someone. Revenge or fear can be even stronger motivators than desire to create something. The anger or fear activate our body and mind and give us energy to act. You should learn how to direct those emotions for your benefit. It is better you use your fear than to fight it.

Ask yourself WHY you want to become rich. If you can find a big enough WHY, which will keep your motivation high, there is nothing that can stop you. Very often I see motivation to get rich based on the responsibility to provide the family.

Why do I want to be rich? Because I have to provide the best for my family. It is not selfish. We will speak more about your motives in latter chapters. You have to find your own WHY.

Another way to get rich quickly is to cheat and squeeze money of your customers, your partners, your employees, citizens or my favorite - to bribe to win tenders for overpriced government orders.

Shortcuts to becoming wealthy – How bribing works

Why would you bribe? It is not the right thing to do, right? Well, if you run a company and the contract is the difference between the necessities to fire your employees, what is the right thing to do? You are responsible for your employees and for the growth of your company and you have to decide if you will give a bribe (let's call it the costs of marketing) and secure the jobs for people who have their families or you will not win the contract and then fire the people. From financial point of view giving a bribe is the same cost as paying for advertising. What is the right thing to do? What do you think? Write me a comment on www.preshovus.com.

I cannot say we have never bribed our business partners to get the better deal. But is bribing really that bad if even governments do it? It can be seen on subventions to companies, which are going to fire their employees. If government wants to keep its unemployment rate low, they can subsidize the company to keep the jobs. Another and much cheaper way that government can keep the unemployment rate low is to change the way they count the unemployed rate. You will exclude some groups of people who are not working from the calculation. By stating they do not want to work. And there it is! Our government just lowered the unemployment rate by 5%. They are economical geniuses, let us vote them again. Have you ever wondered why if you count the unemployment rate and the employment rate you will never get 100%?

Bribe can be seen as the marketing costs. You can bribe by having great social connections and a deformed character - this is of course not what I suggest you to do. But also bribery can be done legally if we call it, for example, lobbying or presents. Everybody likes presents. That is why birthdays and name days were created.

Story about bribing – how it works

Bang! You are caught giving money, for example, to the mayor of your town. You are sitting now in the police office talking to the police officer.

-Of course I was not bribing him. I was giving him money, because we are long term friends and he has a birthday.

-But giving him 10 000 dollars is quite a lot for a birthday present, right?

-No, it is not. We are long-term and very close friends. And actually it is not just a birthday present, because his birthday will be six months from now, but I was also returning him money, which he lent me before.

-He lent you so much money? You sure you have a contract about that large amount?

-We are very close friends and we trust each other, we don't need a contract.

-And you say, there is no connection between the money gift and the fact that your company won a municipal order for 500 new computers, right?

-Right. That is just a coincidence. Anyway, I have here two tickets to this famous and expensive restaurant downtown, but I don't have time to go there, because I lost my time sitting here. I would feel better if the tickets were not wasted. Would you mind helping me and use them yourself?

-How nice of you. I will help you, of course. My wife wanted to go there. Thank you very much. By the way, I have no more questions about your relationship with the mayor. Have a nice day.

And now I want you to imagine that the policeman comes home and tells the story to his wife. What would she tell him, if he had not taken the tickets? All people like gifts, why should the policeman, doctors or politicians be different?

Being a politician makes you rich not because of your salary, but because of your percentage from government orders. Politicians do control cash flow through their budgets and keep a percentage through friendly companies who win government tenders or through bribes. It is easy to spend someone else's money and take a percentage of it. Also, top managers or purchase managers in big companies do that. They use power which they were given to for personal gains. My friend did this for a big company he worked for and because the prices of different companies competing for orders he was managing were almost the same, he chose the best possible supplier and received his bribe as the companies did not know who would win and they wanted to make sure it would be them. My friend is a normal guy and he would be considered silly if he refused such a gift. He had nothing to be ashamed of, because he did the best for his employer as well. He just was the right person at the right place at the right time.

Bankers and politicians have created a system which protects them even if people find out they are taking bribes or that they cheat by taking interests in something they don't even have. If you would sell your car to ten people, you would commit a crime. Banks are allowed to do that legally. Politicians are not allowed to take bribes, but they do. They can do it because they can influence police and judges, so they have protection system against going to jail even when they are caught.

A question for you to ask is – Are those people smart and successful because they fooled the system we live in, or are they just thieves? Who is successful according to your values?

You have to choose your answer for yourself. I am not a judge, I am here to help you to become rich and I have to show you even the dark doors leading to wealth. It is not smart to pretend all people are good and equal. If success in your area is measured only by how much money you can earn, they are truly successful and they should not feel the shame. As money is measurable, more and more people measure success in money and the more money and power you have, the more successful you are in eyes of average people.

There is old saying "All people are equal in the court room. But some of them are even more equal than the others." An excellent lawyer knows all the laws, but the best lawyer knows the jury.

If you want to become wealthy quickly without your own money, you will have to solve someone else's problems or you can use the wealth of someone else. You can win a lottery or marry a wealthy partner. You do not have to create something to become wealthy. What you need is to get and keep control over cash flow. Let's see the bank's example. Banks do control the cash flow, keep a percentage of the money coming in and out, and they loan with interest. What is so special about banks? It is that they are allowed to borrow something they don't even have and make a profit on it. They have, for example, one million dollars, but they can borrow ten millions and that is why they become so wealthy. If they make mistakes, citizens pay for them in taxes as the state helps banks if the politicians receive proper motivation in their bank accounts.

There was a saying in communist regime – **Who does not steal, steals from his own family**. It was meant to steal not from your neighbor but from the company you worked for. As the companies belonged to state, state belonged to you and everything belonged to everyone, you were not considered stealing at all. If you took something, nobody got poorer, but it was considered a crime and it was inspected by police, but from the moral point of view, people did not recognize it as a crime.

It was like with copied music nowadays. If you download an mp3 from the internet and listen to it, have you committed a crime? Yes, you have. But if you never had an intention to buy the singer's CD because of one song you like, will the singer be robbed of something? No, he would not. Money for purchasing the CD was never there. Nothing is missing, so how could he have been robbed? This means people are breaking the laws all the time if they consider what they do is still moral. What is moral depends on the community you live in and on yourself.

There are different moral values in the USA and different ones in Japan. And as people realize there are lots of immoral laws, they are acting more based on their own personal morals then based on the laws. There are so many laws, that the average person can't know them all, so he or she must act based on his or her judgment, not based on laws. That's why politicians, banks or thieves think they are doing nothing wrong. When they feel they are doing something wrong, they can find an appropriate reason to erase that feeling.

Having money is important

In today's oligarch democracy - which is implemented in almost all countries - it is the money which can be the difference between getting the best medical care saving your life or dying on the street. If you are super rich, money can buy you also political, juridical and police cover for anything you have done. Wealth can buy you prestige, increase your attractiveness to the opposite sex, give you power to change world for the better or for the worse. Wealth and money are tools which give you power and it is only up to you how you use them. Money is the same as tools like fire, gun or knife. You can start fire to boil water, make yourself warm or you can use fire to burn your neighbors' house down. You can use a gun to stop criminals or to hunt game for food, but you can use a gun also to rob a bank. You can use knife to cut bread and feed your family or you can use knife to commit a murder. Even dynamite was invented to help people. Money, knifes, guns or fire are just tools. In hands of good people, they can do lots of good things. That's where money and power should be – in hand of good people because all good will be attacked and if good people don't protect good things and values, evil things and values will win.

Ways to get rich even quicker

Marriage or rich partner

Let's take a look on other ways to become wealthy quickly – some women or men still marry for money. It was natural in previous human history until emancipation was invented. As this was done for most of human history, we can consider it normal and moral. The richest families marry to expand or secure their wealth. Look at the members of monarchies or families like the Rothschilds or the Rockefellers.

Women in the past were seeking a partner, who will take best care of her during her pregnancy and during her life. Everybody wants to be loved. We feel we are loved if someone **behaves** the way we expect the person in love to **behave.** It is fair business -> the husband provides for finances and the wife behaves the way which makes him feel loved. In the past, the best partners were the strong and skilled men, so women were falling in love with them. Nowadays it is not about how strong or skilled someone is, but how much money can he afford to spend on children and women. It is not about how much you can earn but how much you can spend on them.

Our western civilization exchanged security of strong arms for financial security. With enough money you can buy the best healthcare, best security enhanced house with private security service, best food, prestige etc. Finding a wealthy partner is another way how to become rich quicker. A good example for this category in my opinion, are women who married e.g. Hugh Heffner. I don't judge them. It may be truth that they married because they fell in love. Probably it was love for the money and the luxury.

Let me tell you a story explaining why you should always stop and think when you receive an "once in a life time" offer. One of my friends asked me what she should do with offer she received from older man. She works at the bar in Prague and he offered her great a job with great pay in London. She was thrilled by the job offer and really wanted it. Offers like this comes to you only once in a life time, right? But then the man told her the price for this job – she has to spend the night with him. She was shocked and refused.

Then she wrote me to get my opinion about whether or not she should do it. She of course had did not tell me in her message she it was she who received this offer, but asked me what I would do if I received an offer like... or other way for her would be to write about her friend who received such offer. But if you can read between the lines, you will understand that it is her who is facing this dilemma. Her colleagues encouraged her to take the offer but I told her not to. I don't know the guy, but from my experience only people who regularly take advantage of other people bad situations, make offers like this. What I told her was that guys like this one have no problem to break their part of the deal without as much as blinking an eye. I did not judge her and the fact that I don't like if someone gets better job or pay rise through the bed, but I focused her attention on the risks. And the risks were high, because I believe that once you will start using your body for financial gains, your reputation will be lost and you will become prostitute. People are various and maybe she would not mind that, but there are other risks. It is possible that the same guy offered this job to ten other girls and *four of them accepted the offer.*

He would have sex with four beautiful women for free – smart guy. Once he had done it, why should he bother about some job in London? What would the girls do if he broke his promise? They could do nothing at all except telling others what the guy did. But would they tell? They would also have to say that they slept with him to get the job, and I believe none of them would want to ruin her reputation at such a young age. Let's assume for a moment that the guy really had the power to give the job to one of the girls he slept with, and he would really give her the job. If he has the power to give someone a job, he probably has the power to take the job away and give it to another willing girl. Would she have to sleep with him regularly to keep the job until he had enough of her and changed her for new girl? Would she be happy knowing that she is in the job just because she behaves like a prostitute?

There is also legal and criminal aspect. What if the guy looks for pretty girls, who are willing to have sex with a stranger for financial benefit or to get a great job? What if, instead of working in London hotel, her ID were to be taken away at the airport, and she were told that the hotel job was no longer available, but that there was another job going, which was also financially attractive. And she would end up in a brothel. That is not the career she wanted, right?

Girls, please, don't be so naive to believe nice stories from strangers. If you really want the job, first get the job and do your part of the deal only after you spent first few days in your dream job. If somebody shows you pictures of a five star hotel it does not mean that the job will be really there. In the best case *scenario you will probably end up working in two star hotels in a foreign city where there is nobody to help you. And that is not what you want, right?*

Becoming famous

There are also famous singers, actors, models or sportsmen who are wealthy. Most of them had to work hard for many years to get where they are now. They had to take risks. If you are passionate about some sport (and you are still young enough, and have predispositions to make yourself elite) go and work hard as they did and you can become one of them. But think also about much more sportsmen who also worked hard, but never made it to the top of their game. The same goes for actors and singers – if you spend ten years practicing something, you also can become elite in it and it will look you are acting or singing with ease. From the average person's point of view, everything these experts do will look easy: its second nature to them, but that means people tend to forget those ten years of hard work.

From my point of view being famous is hard and time-consuming work, just like running a business. But if you are talented and you are passionate about what you do, go for it. It is very rewarding to do what you were born to do and be a world- class success at the same time. In my opinion Will Smith is good example for this category.

How to grow money

If you want to get and stay wealthy you have to accumulate assets. It does not matter if your chosen path is the path of banker, politician, businessman, sportsman or any other way, you still have to accumulate assets to get and stay wealthy. Invest your money or the money of others, and keep control over the assets you gain. Pull out your money as soon as possible and invest in another asset. Repeating this process will make you wealthy as each asset puts more and more money under your control.

Control and cash gain is what makes you wealthy. You can own shares, but if you have no control over dividend payments, you can stay as poor as you were before. You can own the shares but if you do not control company's actions, you don't know if the price of your shares will go up or down. Ownership does not guarantee you income but the **control over the asset is vital**. Once you are the owner, make sure to install control mechanisms to keep the control for yourself.

I learned it the hard way when my former colleague and I started our first company. I put up some money, my colleague put up some and his father invested in our enterprise too. His father did not participate in the business operations, he was just the owner and his shares were controlled by his son. We had a deal allowing every owner to have access to company bank account to control the transactions. However after counting the share in the company, my former colleague decided that he has the biggest share and only he will have access to the bank account. Although we had a written deal, he "wiped his ass with it". Having a signed deal and having power to *bring the other sides to fulfill the deal are two different things.*

The same is applicable to academic education and personal experience, which can tell you very different stories. I have PhD. in economics and I found out first hand that there are many things you will not be taught in school. The most important benefit of academic education is the social network you create while you're at school not the knowledge you will get there.

Let's look at some common myths and truths about wealthy people and money.

Having much money is bad for your health and happiness

No, money is not bad for your health or happiness. It is just a myth. It is not an 'either/or' equation'. You can be wealthy, healthy and happy. What you do, what you eat and the environment you spend your time in is what influences your health, not how much money is sitting in your bank account. Actually, having enough money is good for your health as health care is not free in most countries. Having enough money can be the difference between staying alive or dying. What's bad for your health is the fear or stress of losing money. What's bad for your health is the fear of losing your status among your friends when you lose money. This does not mean money is bad for your health. It means fear and stress is bad for your health. Money is the same as fire. If fire is used properly, it is a very good servant and it can help you to survive. If fire is misused, it can burn your home or a forest. You need to get rid of or to control your fear of not having enough money. It will free you. You are going to die once anyway; so there is nothing to worry about.

If you control your money and not vice versa, there is no threat of becoming ill or less happy if you have money. If you are ill, money can help you to get best possible treatment. If you are not happy, you can use money to change the reason of not being happy as they give you freedom to do what you want to do. You can be poor and happy and you can be rich and happy. I prefer to be rich, healthy and happy.

For the nonbelievers – if you have too much money and it makes you feel miserable, you can always give your money away to someone and your problem will be solved. There will always be someone who will take that burden from you and accept your financial gift. If you want to get rid of your money and have nobody to give it to, give me a call. I like money, I will help you out of your burden!

Hard work and discipline vs. luck and fun at work

You can be hardworking and disciplined businessman or investor and stay behind financially. It is a common situation. It is not how hard you work, but how smart you work. You can work hard on something that is not profitable or not sustainable. My experience is that activities which are the easiest to do and most profitable are the one to focus on. If you choose the right operations, you don't have to work that hard and still receive very high profits with ease. If you are in the right operation and you work hard, it brings you great profits, so hard work in the right operation is much desired.

Hard work in the wrong operation can make you financially comfortable, but unless you dump all the hard work on someone else's shoulders, within a few years you will feel too tired of it and like most other businessmen, you will quit. Owners doing all the work will burn out, if their work is not also their passion. It has been scientifically proven that 90% of all businesses quit within 3 years...

I am just kidding. Don't believe everything that has label "it has been scientifically proven". I have seen various statistics and they showed a quit rate that varied from 40%-90% within first three years. All the statistics show that the quit rate is quite high and there is a higher chance that you will close your business within three years than that you'll last the course. Don't worry, though: even if one of your businesses closes, you can start another business. It is the "death" of legal entities that gets into statistical data, not the 'real life' of your business. Maybe you just had to abandon one legal entity to get rid of the bankruptcy and you used all your knowledge to start another legal entity.

If you can't find out what you are passionate about, I have some good news for you. There are also businessmen who work without the passion, do not work hard and they still become wealthy. You don't need to love your work to get rich. But it will be much easier for you. Those businessman are either very smart, delegating all the work to the right people, or, in some cases, they profit from not keeping their promises or from overpriced government deals.

*My previous business partner's idea of giving a promise was that he had to fulfill his promise only if it suits him and is profitable for him. If the situation changed and you had no leverage over him to make him keep his word, he would say: 'The situation changed and you should know I wouldn't keep my part of the agreement. It's your fault. You know me and you should expect it.' He considered breaking his word and lying a normal situation, and he expected the same behavior from others. It is difficult for me to work with this type of people, but there are lots of businessmen who behave this way. They are very **flexible** with the rules and with fulfillment of deals, so they thrive very often. They are usually very good speakers, promising you whatever you need to hear so that you'll do what they want you to do.*

But don't worry. After some experience you will find out how to identify this type of businessmen. But you will not be able to identify all the people who will take advantage of you. Get used to it that people will try to use you and lie to you when you deal with money or jobs. Don't take it personally, it is natural process.

Discipline is the quality of doing what is necessary to do, when it is necessary to do, whether you like doing it or not. Disciplined action is very necessary for successful operations, whether in business or in your life. It is good to be disciplined and you will have big advantage by being disciplined in life. However I know people who are not disciplined and who still became wealthy. It is better to be disciplined, in my opinion, but discipline is not a necessary quality for getting wealthy. You can be a manipulative speculator without an ounce of discipline and still get wealthy. Or you can have friends who won elections and you can get wealthy even easier, without having to work on your character or skills.

Luck in business is essential. There are so many variables so much that can go wrong, that without at least having some luck, it is impossible to grow a very successful business. For example, sometimes if your customers pay you on time and you have enough money to pay your employees and suppliers in time, you can consider yourself lucky. If your deal is fulfilled by your supplier, and he delivers your order, correctly and on time, you can consider yourself lucky. No one is lucky all the time, so expect that something will ruin your plans. Be prepared.

Our actions are not always caused by positive feelings and motives. Hatred and rage can offer energy for your activities as well, and many times 'bad feelings' can give you even more energy than feelings like love or creative spirit. The problem with anger and hatred is that they should diminish over the long term. Anger is an emotion created to make you act swiftly, decisively and without fear. As soon as the threat or source of anger vanishes, so should the anger. Short term anger is helpful, long term anger damages your health. If you are person who is afraid to start something or you are not a very active person, something bad that happens to you can become a blessing to you. It can ignite your anger and bring you towards the proper action. It is up to you if you use that momentum to create some assets, something with positive influence on your life like exercising or you miss your opportunity to use that energy flow and waste it.

You don't have to enjoy everything you do to become wealthy. It is normal to do activities you don't like, too, because they have to be done. When you build your startup company, you do almost everything by yourself. As soon as the company grows big and profitable enough, it is a good idea to delegate all the work that does not have to be done by you personally to someone who likes that work and is good at it. This delegation of work makes both of you happy. Being wealthy is good for getting rid of activities which you don't like to do, because you can pay someone else to do them. Until you become really wealthy, you have to stay disciplined and be prepared to do things you don't like to do.

Who is more successful in business? Honest people vs. liars, bribers, manipulators

Note: If you don't want to see the real dirty business and keep your ideals clean, skip this chapter. There is big difference between how people should act and how they act in reality. If you wish to increase your lying skill, spend your time with criminals or politicians. Lawyers are good source too – you can learn how to fool people with speaking on the edge of a lie.

„*People are so simple and their desire to fulfill their current need is so high, that a person who wants to lie will always find someone who is ready to be lied to.*"

„*Person who wants to be good and honest at all costs will certainly fail in between people who are not good.*"

Niccolo Machiavelli

If a person is good at social skills, lying and manipulation, he can thrive financially, because there are always new people to be manipulated, used and thrown away. There is nothing like reputation ID to see if the person you just met and you negotiate your first deal with is honorable or not. If this type of person misuses you, you find it out and complain, he can throw you away and find the next person to use. It is that easy for them. There are lots of honorable businessmen. I think most of them are honorable. But even if I would like to think that honor and discipline are prerequisite to wealth, the facts say otherwise. In fact, this is far from the truth.

Many companies I know did not have 'clean' starts and they took advantage of someone else. It is very common and you should not feel bad if you do the same. Former employees taking company's knowledge, customers or database with them when they are leaving and afterwards starting their own business or using it at their next job at your competition is so common, that you have to prepare measures against this even before you hire. But there is not much you can do to prevent this. A lot of companies were started this way, but they will not admit this openly, of course.

If you are not a person of integrity, you can't build long-lasting trust and trust is base of all relationships, but who cares?. Nowadays people change their jobs every few years, so it is sometimes harder to build long-lasting trust and that's why some people feel more "flexible" with keeping their promises. If your customer is a company, it is not the company but the employee of that company who makes purchases from you. And if the person is not also the owner of that company, he asks himself what's in it for him, not just what is in for the company he represents. That's why salesmen use bribes, gifts etc. to get the purchase person to sign the deal.

I have heard from other businessman that in radio broadcasting so called "kickback" is very common with advertisements. The advertiser will pay e.g. 300 000 USD to the radio for the advertisement, but he expects and receives back 150 000 USD in cash. That is also one of the reasons why you can get 50% discount on your advertising when you require no such kickback.

There are many people who exchange their values for enough money, sex or revenge. The employee who thinks that he was lied to by his boss or even conned out of his money will not act in the best interests of the company. If you are just one of many cogs in a big company machine, and you know that company will not be loyal to you if something happens to you, why should you be loyal to the company? If you get a better offer, you change your job the same way as the company will replace you with someone who can do what you do better or cheaper. Lifetime employment is not even a phrase anymore, let alone a career option. If you don't take care of yourself, nobody will.

As an employer do not expect gratitude from the employees for grooming their skills over the years. Don't be a fool. People will work for you as long as it is profitable for them, but they will forget what you did for them the moment they leave you. It is better to be prepared for this moment. It is always better to expect when dealing with money that the other party wants to use you and squeeze you of as much money as they can. And you should do the same if you want to become rich quickly – use other people's resources as much as they allow you to do. Nobody got richer because they were good persons.

Systematic planning vs. intuition and ad hoc problem solving

Some people don't write plans; all they have is a concept of a strategy in their head. Then they adapt the 'plan' to the situation. They are very flexible both the good and the bad senses, and they react to what happens instead of planning. Those people are usually very effective sellers, as they have no problem with promising a potential customer more than is possible. They can then give the order with their promises to someone else. That third party is then obliged to fulfill the contract. If it is not possible to fulfill it, salesman can put the blame on the third party. That can be done repeatedly, over and over again.

Can it be done forever? I believe it can't. But if a salesman's reputation gets so bad and his sales drop so much that it is not profitable for him to stay on the job, he can change industry and start again. In between, he might make a very nice profit for himself and the company he works for, so it can be a win-win situation to have this kind of employee. We can't say they are bad; they are simply different from the fulfilling person. The promise person and the fulfilling person are not compatible long term, usually.

Who is right and who is wrong? It is hard to say and as I already wrote – morality depends on the area and the habits around you. In Europe it is considered the right thing to have only one partner be it wife or husband. In Arab countries it is normal and approved to have more wives. Arabs consider themselves moral with their set of values, and Europeans also consider themselves moral with their set of values. Unfortunately many of those values are not compatible. But let's get back to planning and ad hoc problem solving.

Too much planning can work against you. There is one problem connected to knowing too much, planning too much and thinking too much. It is called **analytic paralysis**. You think and plan too much, but you won't convert those plans and ideas into actions. Without action, there will be no wealth. If you think you have a good plan, act upon it. Don't wait until it becomes 'The Perfect Plan.' There are no perfect plans. It is good to be prepared, but you can't prepare for everything that happens. It is better to act now, based on a good plan, and take corrective actions after the plan A crashes in contact with real world, than to act twenty years from now with 'The Perfect Plan.'

A perfect plan is a myth which does not exist. Just like the perfect market does not exist. They are both academic models used for academic education. The situation WILL be different tomorrow, next month or next year, so there is great probability, that your perfect plan will be outdated the day you start realizing it. If the plan works in principles and can deliver great results, you have enough buffers for that plan to get good results if there is something unexpected. And there WILL be something unexpected along the way. You can count on that.

Planning is very important in my opinion, but you don't need the complete manual for every possible situation when you are starting something. It is not possible to plan everything in advance. Deals or promises from your partners which you included in your plans will be broken and you will have to adapt your plan according to the situation. Some people try to solve any problems which could come into existence, which may be right if you have nothing better to do. But if there is small probability that the problem will arise, are you willing to waste your time and resources on preparing for that problem?

Your time is limited and you have to focus on what is the most important, not on many insignificant problems, many of which will probably never happen. Would spending your week solving possible problems, which will cost your company 100 dollars, be better than spending your week taking advantage of opportunities, which could bring 1000 dollars in sales?

A good plan helps you keep your eyes on your goal and reach the goal in the minimum amount of time. Great goals can be split into smaller ones, and if you divide big tasks into smaller ones, you can achieve anything. Planning is important, but some people manage to get wealthy without any written plan. You have to understand what kind of person you are, what works for you and then use either detailed plans or very vague plans. If you are not sure, try both approaches and measure what works better.

You need talent and charisma to become wealthy

Talent

It is another myth. There are many people out there who are not talented and still are wealthy. Sportsmen are great example. If their approach is to train harder than their competitor, they usually achieve success and if they are in the world's elite at their sport, they achieve wealth on the way up. Talents are not prerequisite for being wealthy. They help, but are not necessary. Some self-made millionaires started from the bottom of society. They had nothing to lose and they had great motivation to get to the elite. If you never had a problem with lack of money when you were young, it is probably that you have not developed the desire for having enough money. This motivation can be based on fear of not having enough money or not having enough power.

Let's compare a talented person who takes his talents for granted, and thinks that he does not have to train that hard because he has a better starting position and better results from the beginning, with a person with less talents but with a burning desire and the discipline to work harder than anyone else. What do we find? Pretty soon the person with strong desire and hard work gets better results than the person with talents. It is because talented people did not have to work that hard: results came to them naturally. They were always the best, so why should they try harder? On the other hand, people without the talents but with strong motives and hard work can rise to the level of talented ones - and they don't stop there. Talent is only 50% of jackpot; the other 50% is the dedication to do what is necessary.

Charisma

Yes, charisma helps when you deal with other people. Today there are lots of millionaires who became rich online. When you are online and you don't see the person eye to eye, charisma is not seen. Of course your brain can make a fictional image of that person even if you have not seen him, and that image in your head can be charismatic based on what he wrote to you, but this is not the real person. It is only your image in your head. Even when you deal with people in person, charisma is what draws people towards you, but you can't keep them working for you just by charisma. Charisma is important for a leader, but to be wealthy, you don't have to be a leader. I repeat - you don't need charisma to become wealthy. Most people work for money, not because they love their leader. Having charisma helps, but it is not essential to run a profitable business.

You need money to become wealthy

Yes, you will need money to become wealthy. Today money is the exchange tool for getting assets. This does not mean you have to own the money yourself. What you need is control over the flow of money. In today's debt-based economy it is smarter to use money put up by someone else to produce cash flow for you. Interest is the price of money and if the price of money you purchase is lower than the price of money you sell, you make a profit. If you can borrow $100 at 10% and use that sum to produce $200, you earned $90 before taxation.

If you need more money than you are able to borrow or earn, you have to create income streams first from other activities. You can learn a skill like computer graphic design, where all you spend is your time and no money; use that skill to earn money by being paid for your services by someone else. This is one way you can lay the foundation of the future investment you desire. Piece by piece, you build your own capital; banks will be more willing to lend you their money as your financial credibility increases.

It costs you no money to start blogging and create income from advertisements. This is how you can build your assets step by step until you have enough money for your dream investment.

You can use control as a leverage to get rich. You can start to control the company you desire by owning as little as 20% of the company, if other owners are not interested in directing the company. Remember - control is more important than ownership. By owning 20% you may be able to control the whole company.

Having the best product or service is the most important thing for having successful business

In an ideal world, where there is the perfect market, being the best would result in you creating a monopoly, because you are the best and your competition can't keep up with you. In the real world you don't have to be the best to get the best deals. You can be a lousy supplier, but with the right connections, friends or bribe at the right place, you can get the best deals. If you know the people who make laws, you can get them to create the monopoly for you. Don't expect you will win just because you are the best. The markets are manipulated and people are manipulated too. This is how oligarchic economies work. The golden rule of economy is: "*He who has the gold, makes the rules.*" As we exchange not gold but money for goods, it is updated to "*Who controls the money supply makes the rules.*"

Small markets, where there is little money to be earned and which are not interesting for the big players, are probably not manipulated, yet. But if there will be a lot of money to be made, there you'll find the sharks, lies and manipulations.

The big question is '*What is most important for success?*' And the answer is '*Find someone who is already successful in what you want to achieve, copy his behavior, improve it if possible and do the same.*' You don't have to start doing something that nobody else has ever done. In my opinion it is better not to do extraordinary things. Best for financial success is to do basic, ordinary things and do the few things that really matter extraordinarily well. Copy what works and throw away everything else. Throw it away even if it is shiny and fancy and everybody is doing it. You don't have to follow the crowd.

Many people I know are waiting for the perfect product to start a business. They keep waiting for ten years. I believe that they must have seen at least one perfect product during that time, but they got used to the waiting and missed the opportunity. You can have the best product in the world and end up broke. But there are others who started their actions and found the perfect product on the way. One of central European TV companies which is called Markiza, started in business by producing nylons and pantyhose. Later they changed their core business, becoming the leading TV station in Slovakia. It is easier to start moving and then to find the best product or alter your core business; don't procrastinate. Do something even if it will end with failure and you will have to switch to something more profitable. The first step is the hardest, and then with momentum at your back you will be able to find the solution.

For mainstream markets you have to use profitable marketing. How you sell something becomes more important than what you sell and as much as 50% of your costs can be spent on marketing. Even with a product that isn't very good, you will learn how to sell: and being able to sell profitably is the most important ability when running a business. Sales create cash flow and cash is the lifeblood of business. There are some world-class companies which operate with minimum marketing costs. They use only word of mouth and PR marketing. Usually these operate in niche markets and already have strong brand identity and solid reputations.

I am a loser, I will never be wealthy

Yes, that is the truth. If you consider yourself a loser, your subconscious mind will make you behave like a loser. Until you change your mindset, you will be a loser. What you have to do is to build up your self-confidence and experience small successes. Start with small goals and achievements by doing what you like and what you are good at, then build your self-esteem. Erase words like *I am loser* or *I can't do it* from your vocabulary. Go to the chapter on brain programming first. If you think you can't get wealthy, you are right, you can't. I can't help you. You are the only one who can help you.

I know of a successful businessman who was a depressed loser when he was young. He hated the real world and took refuge in fantasy books, where heroes dedicated their time to becoming strong and powerful. He wanted to be like them. Then something happened and he refused to live in fear and he changed his life. The good news for you is that if he could change from loser to winner, you can do it too. It took him 3 months to change. To find more about how he changed after one incident that burned in his blood with anger read my book about him - From loser to hero – Confession of former fighter. I believe it will inspire you. Visit www.preshovus.com/from-loser-to-hero for more information.

You can change who you are now, even if you are an alcoholic, a murderer or a rapist. Maybe you deserve the death penalty for what you did, but you can still behave like a good man at least in your last moments of life.

You will always be responsible for what you did and you are responsible for what you will do today. If you don't know what you should do to change yourself, start by serving other people. You have to really want to change yourself and behave like the person you want to become. That it is not an easy task. There is no place for words like *I would like to change, but I will do it tomorrow*. If you really desire it, you will do it **now**.

Stay humble and start with small steps, but start now. Use waves of energy that motivates you whether it is joy, desire or fury. Every person alive has necessary energy to adapt to his surroundings and this means you have it too, even if you don't know it. All you need is to do is to focus, find it and use it. If you really can't find it, you can seek out extreme situations and once you are cornered like animal, the animal in you will wake up. If you can't motivate yourself to do something and nothing works for you, you can start by creating a situation where you will have no other option than to start or die. You can make life harder for yourself and it will make you stronger.

What to do if you feel like a loser

Do you feel angry right now because your life is not going the direction you would like? Let's handle your anger first.

Long term anger is bad for your health, but temporary anger is a feeling pumping you up with energy and decisiveness. Revenge is also good for your survival. If somebody cheats you or beats you, you should take appropriate steps preventing him from doing it again. Usually, after you hurt them back badly enough, they will find an easier target next time. Of course you should do it smart and not break the law with your actions. That's why you have to understand your negative emotions and learn how to control them.

I know it is not easy, but the breath control techniques or sports will help you with that. There are many efficient martial arts which teach you how to breathe. If you feel like a loser right now, I recommend you try active sports or martial arts. Life is a fight and you have to learn how to fight. We will make a winner from you!

Of course fighting sports are not for everybody. You can try different sports or arts. What is essential is that by practicing it you will feel how you are fighting to reach your goal and feel energy coming with the victory. Winning will teach you about self-esteem and loses will teach you about humility. If you don't achieve those feeling even after few months of practice, try something else.

In my opinion and experience a man should know how to fight at least with words when not with fists. The world out there is not nice to the weak and you have to know how to fight back. After being taken down, you have to rise again to your feet and fight back. This is the winner's attitude and you have to experience that. You will never get that experience from just reading books, but only through action and pain. Get out of your comfort zone and soon your comfort zone will become broader. You will do things you thought you were not able to do and as it becomes your habit, you will do them with ease. It is beautiful feeling to look back and see what you have done even though a few months ago you thought it impossible for you.

I recommend you the practice of martial arts because you will learn to be disciplined and dedicated. If you will be put down a hundred times, you will rise a hundred times and continue to fight. Winners don't give up. It is O.K. to change your approach, activities or direction to reach your dream, but don't give up on reaching it. It is O.K. to ask yourself if that dream is worth all the trouble. And sometimes your answer will be no, it is not worth it. If you find out that your dream is not worth the effort, you have to look inside yourself to find your real dream. Your real dream will be worth the effort. It is the reason you live – to fulfill that dream. You will know it is The Dream when you will know deep inside that you are ready to die for it.

In the past boys were going on difficult errands before they were awarded with the signs of manhood. They got hurt in the process or they even died. But they became real men when they succeeded. We are having such great lives, that we grew soft. We are no more trying to reach our adulthood because we don't want to get hurt. Fear rules our lives instead of courage. This is what distinct the men from boys and adult women from girls. Once you will learn to handle your fears by overcoming them or by making a deal with your fear, you will grow and will gain great gift. The gift of knowing that you will do whatever will be necessary to reach your goals or die trying.

For improving your winning attitude read my book – From Loser to Hero.

Here is an example which worked for me: I was not satisfied with the progress I have made in writing this book. I turned off the internet and the cell phone to eliminate disturbances, and then I worked on the book faster and more effectively. When the evening came and I was still not satisfied with my progress because I hadn't spent my time productively, I used the Spartan technique. I removed luxury from my life like sleeping on the bed or using hot shower until I was satisfied with the results. Sleeping on a sleeping mat will make you wake up early, because it is not so comfortable and you will sleep only as long as your body has to sleep. Cold shower will make you healthier and stronger too. It is not pleasant, but it will wake you up instantly.

What I usually do is to exchange bed for a sleeping mat and sleeping bag and sleep on the floor. I love sleeping in comfortable bed so much that sometimes I take an hour to get out of bed. Then I do my morning exercise and eat breakfast before I start to work on the book. Sleeping on the floor helps me to get up early because the floor is really not comfortable. Usually when I am sleeping on the floor, I sleep for only four to six hours a night, instead of sleeping seven hours in bed and then spending another hour just lying there not wanting to move my feet from the warm blanket to the cold floor.

Then I drink coffee or energy drink to keep me awake, which is not healthy, but it is good for the '*I will do whatever it takes*' approach. If you drink coffee or energy drink, make sure they are quality products without toxic ingredients like e.g. sugar free aspartame and don't pass the daily intake limit. Also, make sure you do physical exercise to balance your mental work.

I haven't heard of anybody who died because of lack of sleep so far. Some people die of an heart attack caused by being overworked, but they don't die because of lack of sleep. They die, because their heart can't stand the thought of not being the best as they are expected to be, fear of losing money, losing their face, their power is what kills them. If they would accept and love themselves as they are, it would not happen to them.

A few days a month with only four hours of sleep a night are alright for a healthy person. Another part of the Spartan technique is postponing your meals until you reach planned result. Hunger motivates you to work efficiently, and don't worry – one day a week without the food will make you healthier. We don't need to eat as much as we do eat. That is why I keep some fat on myself to be able to work for few days even if I had no time to eat. It is natural for animals not to find food for few days – that is why fat was created. Fat will help you during 'no food' periods. If your body has no fat at all I advise you to get some.

Another example of using Spartan technique to shape your character I read was how one guy from Czech Republic and other people from all around the world had to pee in big pot during their whole day running to control their hydration. Instructors told them, they will drink the contents of the pot in the evening. When he saw filthy penises of other warriors, he had to think about all the illnesses their urine possessed. He could not imagine that he would be able to drink this urine. But in the evening his ego was broken and he drank it. After such character building experience he understood that there is nothing he can't do. The only limits to his results are the limits he sets himself. That is the truth – if your ego can handle it, you can handle it too.

I like Systema martial art and its principles as it helps to develop the real warrior in you. A good warrior is handy in combat, his spirit is strong and his body is healthy. The body must be free from tension and then it is tireless, flexible and explosive. The psyche is calm, without anger, irritation, fear, self-pity, self-deception, and without pride. The warrior who is like this controls his ego and there is nothing he can't accomplish. Most of us are economic warriors fighting the competition in our jobs, but we can learn the lessons from the soldiers too.

The customer is always right

No, the customer is not always right. Sometimes customers are wrong and sometimes they even lie. But even if they do, you can't treat them as liars. You have to call some external authority to judge the problem and give facts to the customer. Never tell him he is lying, because he would lose his face and get angry. Just show him the facts and tell him you are sorry, but you are obliged to act based on those facts.

Remember that your company must be profitable to stay in business. And also every customer must be profitable for you. If your customer stops being profitable for you, keeping him would mean a loss for the company you have to 'fire' him. It makes no sense to have customers who make you a loss instead of a profit. If you consider your service to be above average compared with your competition and you can live without that customer, direct him to your competitors. You will increase your profitability and lower the profitability of your competition with a bad customer. Create black lists of customers who complain all the time. It is better for you and it is better for them because angry complaining is not good for their health. With your bad customers gone, you will have more time for your good customers.

Think also about your employees. If blacklisted customer is persuading your employees that your service is bad, it affects all other customers who are in contact with that employee, because your employee's trust in your product is reduced. It reduces the morale of your employees if they have to listen to stories about how bad your services or your products are. Then you have to remind them that the percentage of satisfied customers is much higher than those who complain. By keeping bad customers, you will lower your overall customer service. If your employee has to spend most of his time with unreasonable customers, there is less time to spend with good customers. If your employee's attitude is poisoned by bad customers, he will give worse service to other customers. Get rid of bad customers immediately while allowing them to keep their face. Support your employees if in conflict with a customer. You are in the same boat with your employees.

Money will change your character and you will become a bad person

It is just another myth. If you understand what money is and have control over it, you will be able handle your emotions and character even if you're rich. You don't have to change your character because you have lot of money. If you wish, you can leave it in your bank account and live the same simple life as you lived before.

On the other hand, money **could** change your character if you don't have control over it. The amount of money you use affects your social status and social status affects your character. If you are very poor, it is highly probable, that you will spend your time with other poor people. The majority of poor people do not plan for a bright future - often they do not plan at all. If you are constantly in a group of people who do not plan and make fun of you if you do plan, you will be affected by them. It is up to you whether you conform to people around you and start behaving like they do, or whether you follow your own path, no matter of what others say about you.

Sometimes a man who becomes rich realizes his increased value for other people and he changes his opinion about himself. His wealth can change his habits too, and habits affect the character of a man. If you have a lot of money, you have power over many people, because you can buy their services. Some people who got rich without work e.g. by inheritance, can have the false belief that they can 'buy' other people, and they can become arrogant. It is true that they can buy what other people will do. The problem starts when they believe they can buy anybody, which is false. Not everybody is interested in their money. If you are rich, you have to be able to recognize who can be bought and who will be offended by your behavior. People are different and you have to treat them differently and with dignity unless you want to see the back of them. People are not equal even if I would like to believe they are.

The blessing of having enough money is that you will no longer have to worry about your personal physical needs. The curse of being rich and showing it to others is that people around you know you are rich, and you may not be able to tell who really loves you and truly cares about your well-being and who spends his time with you just because of your money. Many rich people then change their behavior to protect themselves, and assume that everybody is with them just because of their money until they prove otherwise. Three main solutions are: 1. Get used to the fact that some people will be with you because of your money. You have to learn how to separate those two kinds. 2. Do not show off that you are rich. Then you will be not attractive to people who seek to use you because of your money. 3. Spend your time with people who were your friends before you got rich.

Most self-made millionaires who became rich by their hard work live below their means, and they decided to **sacrifice luxury today to enjoy freedom tomorrow**. This sacrifice shaped their character, but in a good way. They were affected by what they did and not by the amount of money in their bank account.

There are cases of lottery winners who continue to work at their jobs and live in the very same houses they had before they struck it lucky. Money did not change them. There is nothing wrong with being wealthy. Money is just a tool. It can be used for good and also for bad purposes. It is up to you how you use it.

You can become wealthy only by looking wealthy

This was true for a long time. Now the rules have changed slightly. Whether you need to look wealthy or not depends on how you make money. If you do business where your partners see you, it is important that you look and dress the part. As a manager, you should dress appropriately when dealing with other people. There are some generally accepted exceptions like IT industry. When two IT guys are dealing face to face and they both do not care about dress code, it is acceptable not to wear conventional business clothes. But when the same IT guy needs to visit the bank to get a loan, he should wear business clothes. You have to make good first impression on people who will influence whether or not you will get your loan.

There are people who work only through internet and communicate through e-mail or chat. You can manage results of your team through internet and also get your loan approved without visiting bank in person. If nobody sees you, it is not important how you look, right?

No. It is not complete truth. There is always one person who does see you. He is always watching. Clothes you wear influence your self-image. Even if you work from home, it is good idea to change your clothes during your working hours. This will help you to switch to 'working mode' and back.

I am too old to become wealthy

There are multiple examples of people starting their own business in their old age who succeed. Everybody probably knows the story of Ray Kroc purchasing McDonald's in his fifties and turning it into a worldwide success story. Most self-made millionaires became millionaires only after they were fifty years old.

If you are old and you were an active person during your younger years, you should have now quite a big network of contacts and experience. Maybe your old friend is a director in the bank or has an influential post in politics or the tax bureau. With more time spent on networking, your contacts can be of higher quality.

Experience is gained by actions and time. If you are older and you spent your time well, it is probable, that you experienced many problems and learned how to solve or avoid them. You may lack the energy of a younger person, but you can catch up by being more effective and focused. As an older and more experienced person, you probably went through painful mistakes already and you will not repeat them again. If you are older, probably your children are grown adults and you don't have to take care of them anymore. This means more energy which you can use for your business.

First you have to save money

Saving and budgeting are good habits and you should practice them. It helps you to control your money and your cash flow. For generations it was safer to invest only money you had already earned and saved. This approach is very low-risk even today.

If you want to be rich and you are not owner of large capital already, you will have to learn how to use the money of other people and use it as leverage with your money, your time, your knowledge and your actions.

When you borrow money, you take the risk of not being able to pay it back with interest. This risk must be legitimated with potential profit and your limited liability. Cost of money (interest rate) must be lower than your final profit rate after taxation. If you borrow money at 10% interest rate, your profits must be higher than 10% to be able just to pay your loan back. Having 0% profit and taking risk is not smart. The minimum profit when taking business risks should be 30%, depending on how big the risk is and how much of your energy you need to put into that business or trade. Profit rate should include enough reserves for unplanned costs. There are always some unplanned costs in business.

For big investments it is not realistic to use your savings for financing. Think twice before taking a loan, but don't be afraid of it. Don't let your emotions guide you when preparing the business plan. Use limited liability company to protect yourself if everything goes wrong and you have no business and no money to pay your loan back.

Live below your means and be frugal

Just because you can afford to buy something, it doesn't mean you should. First of all you need to define what your financial limits are. Make a budget and stick to it. Common sense tells us that you should spend only so much as you have earned during that time frame. You can set year, month or week as a time frame for your budget. I use year and monthly budgets.

If you want to be rich, you have to live below your means, but you don't have to be frugal. If you live above your means, there is no money left to invest and without investing in assets you can't get rich. If you earn $1000 and spend $800, you live $200 below your means. If you earn $2000 and spent $1500, you live $500 below your means. The best option would be to earn $2000 and spend $800. You will then keep $1200 for your investments. It is how much money you are able to keep. If you don't want or are not able to spend less, you have to focus on earning more. The fastest legal way to riches is running your own business. It is hard to get credit from the bank if you are just starting and that is why you have to save money for your later company. Most people simply are not that lucky to get a credit from someone.

Being frugal is about **delayed gratification**. If you save money, but never invest it, you are not using money as a tool. Saving makes only sense when you save to purchase something. The best usage of money is for keeping you safe, healthy, properly clothed and fed. If your physical needs are met, then the best usage of your money is for purchasing assets and then using cash flow from your assets to have some fun and purchase more assets. If you delay your gratification **and** purchase assets, you are on your way to financial freedom. If you just delay your gratification without specific goal in mind, you are usually losing your money because of the inflation tax.

Most people I know either focus on earning more money or on spending less. My father focuses on spending less. Spending less is good to the point where you refuse to spend your money on assets to avoid the risks. The problem with my father's approach is that he prefers to take no action at the present time to get rich. Instead he says 'I should have invested into XY in 1990,' or at some other time in the past. Then he is unhappy that he did not invest.

When interesting investment occurs, he is so cautious he will not invest or take action. On the other hand I have to tell you that during 6 years I have lost more money than he did during 30 years. But also during those 6 years I have made more money than he did during his 30 years. We are simply different when we invest. He is guided by fear of loss and I am guided by vision of gain.

If I have to choose between spending less and earning more, I choose to spend less and earn more. It is another 'either/or' myth. You can both spend less and earn more. But if there were only those two options and I had to choose between earning more and spending less, I would choose earning more. If you are busy earning more money, usually there is almost no time to spend that money because you are so busy. I do not believe in fanatic saving money by being too frugal, but if you are very busy, you will not have time to buy unnecessary things which you will not use. You will step out of mass consumption area in your mind which we are programmed by watching TV ads, billboards etc. Those ads are created to make you want to buy things, you will not use after few months. I know it, because I have been working in the advertisement industry myself. All you need is a warm place to live, food and water, few clothes and shoes to protect you from the environment, means of transport (feet, bike or public transport is the best option in big cities) and tools needed for your work and study. That's all. Everything else is just wants, not needs.

I know some people who will travel halfway across town to save a few cents in a sale, but what they do not realize is that they spent more on their fuel, and they bought more goods in multi-packages than they really need. They lost more than they saved. What they do is wasting money and goods, which they will throw away. But more important, they also waste their time. If they didn't use their time on chasing good deals, they could use it to earn more money. They keep more money if they earn $50 extra during that time, than if they save $20 in sale. Those people usually don't take their time into account in their saving equation, and think their own time is free, so they have lost nothing of value. This is not true. Our time is limited. Each day we have only 24 hours and we can't use that time anymore if it is spent on shopping. Choosing how you will spend your time each day will make you either successful or not successful. **Your time is limited, your money is abundant.** You can always earn new money but you can't turn back the time.

Use the approach which works for you to get the maximum amount of **money you will keep in the end**. It is both about earning as much as you can and spending as little as you can.

Good advice to help you stop purchasing rubbish is to *act as if 'You can't throw it away once you purchase it.'* If you set your mind to '*I will have to keep it, do I have a spare place to put it in?*' You will stop purchasing garbage that gets thrown away anyway. Shop for quality items that will last longer and buy them only if you are sure you will use them. Sell your old items which you don't use before you purchase a new toy.

"Buy only what is necessary, not what is convenient. What is unnecessary, even if it only costs one cent, is expensive." Seneca

You have to keep yourself and your finances under control

Managing yourself is more difficult than managing your finances. If you want to get rich and stay rich, you have to learn both managing yourself and how to control your finances by budgeting. First of all, start tracking your spending. Later you will find ways to pay less in taxes, but for now just record your spending, to have exact data on how much you spend. If you are doing it already, you may be surprised how much you spend on items you don't really need.

Tracking your spending is crucial for stopping money leaks from your purse. Most women I know have the ability to spend everything they earn or receive from their husband. It is difficult to explain to them that they don't have to have zero in their account by the end of month. Having your spending under control is so crucial that you should stop thinking about it and just do it automatically. When you use your plastic money or online bank account, it is easy for you to summarize your spending. Keep all receipts of your purchases and use them for your financial report. Keep track of everything you spend your money on. Yes, I mean everything. Do it at least for few months and then for a month each year to see if you still keep it under control.

Keep track of what interest rates are paid for having your money on your bank account and how much you pay for your debts. Look for better interest rates and use them. Find leaks in your money system and close them. Don't let your money leave you if it is not necessary. Don't be lazy: fix the leaks.

Don't rent, buy

For some items it is good advice, for some items it is not. If you purchase items that grow in value (real estate is good example in the long-term, even if the last few years seem to show us otherwise), it is better to purchase it. After some years you can sell it with profit. Or with loss. Prices can go up or down so remember to purchase them when they are cheap and sell when they are expensive. You will have to go against average market decisions and the bigger investment you plan to execute, the more time spent analyzing the investment is necessary.

There is no general advice whether it is better to buy or rent. You have to calculate it each time you make a purchase decision. With this calculation you delay the purchase and have more time to think whether you really need that item. We often feel that we simply need that item and our emotions persuade our rationality quite easily. Emotions always win over the rational if you don't control them. You can purchase small items based on emotions to feel temporarily better, but when there are expensive items at stake, take your time, cool down your emotions and act rationally. If you can direct and control your emotions in negotiation, you will have unfair advantage over most people, because most of people are guided by emotions.

If you are going to ski for example and you are thinking about purchasing second-hand skis for $100, because you don't need the brand new ones, think again. How often will you use those skis? Will you even have time to use them? Will they not just stand in your garage and take up your limited garage space?

Compare it to borrowing brand new skis for $5 a day for ten years and your free space in the garage. That would make also $100 over ten years, if you ski only two days a year. But over those ten years you can use remaining $90 to invest and earn more money. If you invest your $100 well and you receive $10 profit every year, you get your ski experience for free. Profitable borrowing is very usable for items that lose value over time. If item is appreciating its value over time, it is generally better to buy it. O.K. I know we have to buy some doodad from time to time, but let's control this spending and use it to your advantage. If you purchase smaller doodad as a reward after earning a lot of money, I fully support your idea. Making money should be rewarded.

Remember: What you should seek when investing is control. If you can't control the asset, don't buy it.

I don't need to write down plan, I have it in my head

This is what I hear very often from people who ask me about how to improve their financial condition. If I persuade them that a written financial statement and spending report is needed, usually they are surprised how much they throw away on things they don't need. You should keep track of all your spending for at least a year to understand yourself better. This will help you, when planning your spending for next year, to be more realistic. Budgeting and planning is crucial.

Don't just read about it, really do it. If you don't track your spending and don't plan your income, stop reading and do it now. It doesn't have to be some highly sophisticated table. All you need is a sheet where you divide your spending into groups and enter each expense you incur. I believe that some people don't do it because they fear the numbers will show how much they are wasting and they know they will feel bad when they see the truth. Don't be afraid of the truth. True information is your friend.

More about financial reporting and planning in the chapter *Accounting, numbers and analyzing assets*.

Time is money

Well, time is not money if we take it literally, but time and money are very important aspects of man's life. If you use your time well, you can earn more money and accumulate assets. Time and money are almost bound together. People are spending money to save time and people are spending their time to earn money.

Lot of people say 'If I had more time, I would start ...' You can put in anything from 'my own business' to 'take better care of my body.' The basic fact is that you will never have more time. Each day has 24 hours; you can't have 25 or 30 hours a day. Sometimes we wish we had less time. Usually it is when we are bored or tired and we wish to stop the activity we are doing right now. This means time is constant and only our perception of time changes. Learn how to achieve more in less time.

What you do with your limited time is the difference between yourself being wealthy or poor. **Procrastination is your enemy**. The older you get, the more you realize your limited time on this world. Use that time well; don't waste what you have been given as a gift. Be strict with yourself about your time usage at work. Don't spend ten minutes on a call that can reach its goal in two minutes. Use your time as effective as you can. If you can get your work done in 5 hours instead of 8, you just "earned" 3 free hours extra for that day. You can spend those 3 hours on something you like doing. And you would like to study how to increase your assets, right?

Ask yourself "How much is my hour worth? " If your monthly income is $1000 and you work 100 hours a month, then your hour is worth $10. Can you get someone else to do the tasks which take you 50 hours a month and $400? If you can, great: you just saved 50 hours and $100. On the other hand, you will keep only $600 in the end if you don't use those 50 hours for earning money. If you use them for work in which you are specialized and you will get paid $15 an hour, you earned an additional $750. This makes your income $1350, and your income increased by $350. It is not as easy in reality as it is written in this example, but it is possible. Look for opportunities you have around yourself and in yourself for more effective usage of your limited time.

The richer you will get, the higher value will have your time for you. Constantly ask yourself *"What is the best usage of my time?"* Behave like rich people and you will become one. Would you spend a few days travelling by car from L.A. to New York or would you use a plane, if your hourly worth is $1000? What would the rich do?

There is no limit to how much money you can make and that is why money is not scarce. Time is an entrepreneur's most precious resource, because it is the only thing that truly is scarce. Your time is more important than your money. You can always earn more money, but you can't earn more time. Time is limited, time is precious. What you can buy, is your free time. If you pay someone to do the work for you, you can use that time for what you want.

You may have heard of Parkinson's Law. It is often used in reference to time usage: the more time you've been given to do something, the more time it will take you to do it. It's amazing how much you can get done in twenty minutes if twenty minutes is all you have. But if you have all afternoon, it would probably take way longer. Overload yourself with work and you will learn how to do more in less time.

You have to be innovative and creative to become wealthy

This is our next myth. Sometimes people are confused by terms innovation and creativity. The simplest definition of innovation I am comfortable with is '**Innovation** is intended change, which brings improvement.' Innovation and improvement is very good for business, because it can give you competition advantage over other companies. This is true, if you and your competitors are on the same level in the beginning. Innovation in business, as it brings desired changes, will lead to better results of that company. Innovation is great and desired but it is not necessary for business operations. There are businesses which operate in traditional activities and because of their monopoly, they don't have to evolve. Innovation helps you to get rich more quickly and I strongly advise you to look for possible innovations. Some authors call it a leverage.

To use innovation you don't have to be innovative yourself. You can copy innovation from your competition. All you have to do is watch your competition and if they change something (e.g. a competing bank starts to offer on-line banking), you can test it yourself and measure if it is innovation for you. If it brings no improvement in performance for you, it is not innovation. If online banking lowers your profit margin because you receive less money in fees compared to regular bank account, it is not innovation for you. Using your online banking can still be innovation for your online customer, because he saves time and money. But if it is not profitable for the bank, the bank can't call this change innovative. If you can't measure the benefit, you can't call it innovation.

Other related myth is that you have to be the first on the market to apply the innovation. There are multiple cases where the first innovator spent much too money on testing what works and what does not before he found the innovation. After he found it, others copied it from him with much smaller costs. I don't say it is nice, but it is the reality and it is done all the time all over the world. Copying is easier than finding innovations and that is why it was, it is and it will be done whether we like it or not. It is natural. We can see it even with the penguins. First to jump off the cliff takes highest risk that orca will eat him. If others see that he is alive, they will jump the cliff too. But nobody wants to be the first. The first one can be eaten. Good example is Google. There were other search engines before Google, but it is Google which is the market leader now. You don't have to start first to become the winner.

Creativity is the ability to create something new. Not everything newer is better than what was created earlier. You can be creative and lose money. You can be conservative and earn money. In many cases creativity 'kills sales.' Good marketing measures how much money is spent on a certain activity and how much sales and profit it brings.

If you use an advertising agency, and I was witness to this many times, you and your agency have different goals most of the time. You want to increase sales profitably and spend as little as possible, while the agency wants to spend as much money as possible and then take a percentage of that advertising budget. For the agency it is good to be well known and their partial goal is to create 'creative advertisements' which will win some advertising awards so they can promote their agency through the award. Many times the agency is satisfied if they make your brand more known or if their ad gets more views. What agencies will not tell you is that there is a big difference between what people like to see (creative advertisement) and what makes them buy (classical boring but tested and measured advertisement). Creativity can have negative influence as well. Not everything that is new is better. You have to measure and test it to be sure.

As you can see, innovation or creative innovation is good for business, but it is not necessary to be innovative or creative yourself.

Lot of authors write that you need just one idea to get rich. Having a great idea is just small step to get rich. The idea itself has no value. Everybody has ideas. My friend has list of 100 ideas on which he will base his businesses. So far he has a job and no business, because he lacks actions to realize those ideas. There are ideas everywhere and it is not difficult to choose one idea that will make you rich if you **implement it successfully**. To implement the idea successfully is the important part of the sentence. The successful people are not the one with the ideas, but those who implement those ideas. Those who have strong will, endurance and decide to risk failing when trying to realize the idea. And when they fail, they have courage to start again.

Spending time with your boss can increase your salary more than excellent performance

At my job as sales manager I was quite happy for the first three years. I managed to persuade my second boss to be paid a percentage of sales and I managed to increase the sales each year by more than 100%. Everyone was motivated and I was able to build a small and efficient team. In three years I had, together with my team, profitably increased sales from 20 000 € a month to 120 000 € a month. We had a great mentor in Slovenia and our new boss in Slovakia was a miracle. At least for the first year, he was the perfect manager and a leader. I admired him and wanted to be like him. He was young, ambitious, competent and efficient. The right person in the right place. Everything looked great for more than a year.

Then he added one person to my team without my approval. It was done because our super boss did not have the heart or balls to fire her. She was not the right person for the job. She never wanted the job and she lacked the needed skills. She took the job just because she did not want to leave the company. I reported her lack of ability and motivation multiple times and asked my boss to let me fire her, but I was refused. In the end, after few months he agreed, but my department lost the potential sales during that time.

Days were passing and our boss had changed completely after his year and a half at the company. He was my fourth boss at that company as none of them lasted very long. He stopped coming to the meetings on time or stopped coming at all. He stopped replying to e-mails, and our work was blocked because we were waiting for his approvals. He was breaking his promises and we began to make fun of him behind his back. He never explained this change, but we thought that the company system broke his will and he realized he was just a puppet in his boss's hands.

What triggered me to give up that job was lack of respect and my boss's time management. That day we agreed on meeting at 10:00, but he had no time, so he told me that he would call me later. I understood that he had more important tasks to do, but I didn't understand why was he not able to cancel or re-schedule our meeting if he had no time for it. I asked him more than three times if I should wait, or if we should change the date of the meeting. I always got the response to wait.

So I waited until two o'clock and then left for a lunch. At 16:30 I was given a call to meet him and my consultant from Hungary. Because I had to leave at five p.m., I told them we would have to finish by that time. Of course we did not. It was because my boss had lots of detailed questions. At five I told them that I had to leave. My proposal was refused of course, and I was told to stay. I had to leave as I was teaching at 17:30 at university, so I told my boss that I am sorry, but he is four and half hours late for this meeting and I can't stay, because I have a meeting where 24 people would be waiting for me and they would come on time. I still consider it a good decision and I would do it again. Being 4.5 hours late without saying he was sorry and understanding that I couldn't wait that long for him and couldn't change all my other responsibilities just because he was late. What he did is quite rude in my eyes. I was told to stay, but I left.

My Hungarian consultant apologized to me the next day by e-mail, but it was not his fault. My students came on time and we had our class. It was one of my hardest decisions in my life, but I have never regretted it. Actually I am proud of the fact that even if I knew it will be harmful to my career, I did what was the right thing to do.

I was given another guy to my team, but it was a strange situation because he reported directly to my boss and not to me. As I had no decision rights over him I told my boss that I do not accept responsibility for this guy's results. Responsibility goes in hand with control. One does not work well without the other. The guy spent half of his time in the boss's office and his productivity was extremely low. An example of his results is that he spent two weeks arranging a 50% discount on advertising on one well known website called azet.sk. He came back to the office as a champion because of this result and wanted to be treated as hero. What he considered to be an extraordinary result, I considered it to be under performance. I had done the same deal one year before in two hours and I also received free lunch from the sales manager of that website.

The morale in my team grew bad as this new guy earned more than any one of us did and he refused his tasks by simply saying that he did not know how to do it. He was not sharing the team workload, he had benefits we were not allowed to have and still earned more than we did. As the hostility between my boss and me grew the situation got tense. My bonus system was only written in e-mail and not updated to the contract for three years so it was possible to stop paying my bonus percentage from money which I earned the company. And this is exactly what happened.

Our bonuses were paid every three months and without being told anything, I received one fifth of what I was supposed to receive in my bank account. I thought it is just an accident because I delivered very satisfying results to the company and the sales grew as they should. I spoke with my boss and he told me that I would not get the money because he was not satisfied with my work.

Later I was told that part of my money was given to the new guy. I did not care about the arguing that he had new baby and a wife to finance. This meant it is not as important what results you deliver to company you work for, but how much time do you spend in your boss's office asking him for a pay raise in that company. I was very angry and tried to get that money for three months. I got something back but I made the decision that nobody would "steal" my money without being punished. Then I spoke with one of my colleagues about options of how to monetize our knowledge and we decided to start our own company.

Lesson learned: *If your agreement is not written in a legal contract, the other party does not have to fulfill its obligations. It does not have to be fulfilled even if it is written as I learned later, but your chances are better if it is written and signed.*

Until you have your money in your pocket, they are just a promise.

Basic types of rich people

Think about your role model, your current financial status, actions and attitude towards getting rich. There are various ways to get rich. If you like the lottery winner approach, you will find some good advices here. You can even try to inherit wealth even if you are not from rich family. You can try to marry a millionaire or do the illegal stuff. Only you are responsible for your actions and will carry a tag on your forehead for what you do. Choose wisely and carefully. But on the other hand – if you become very rich even the illegal way, people's hearts will soften for you if they can earn something of your riches. People tend to forget and forgive if it is profitable for them.

If there is a gold rush, some people will try their luck and will dig for gold, but some people will try their brain and will start to produce and sell shovels.

Which type rich person is closest to your soul?

Lottery winner

The easiest way for an average person to get rich is to win a lottery. It is also one of the most improbable ways. Odds that you win a million dollars are so low, that it makes no sense to take it seriously. It is based on luck and lottery luck can't be repeated. It is all right to try your luck with a small amount of money, but don't really expect to win. It can be fun and thrilling to watch the lottery draw, but take it more like a ticket to the cinema than a realistic way to get rich. Unless you have an insider at the draw that will draw your ticket, there is no way to control the outcome of a lottery. If you can't control and influence it, it is usually just a waste of your time.

Proven ways to get rich are those, where you have control over the outcome of your actions. If you won a big amount of money, learn how to invest it slowly after you are sure of what are you doing. Before you know what to do with the money, it can take a year or two to find an investment where you will not lose all your money quickly. Good advice is to keep your mouth shut and split the money in parts. Keep only as much money as you have spent for last 12 months and put the rest into an account where you can't take it and spend it easily.

Live your life without huge changes before you decide which investment is suitable for you. Start the process of learning how to manage money, start budgeting and saving. Don't spend much more money than you did last year before you won. It is O.K. to spend more, but spending more than 150% of the amount you spent the year before you won is risky. Your biggest concern must be not to lose that money in risky investments and not to attract people who will 'help' you with your money. You don't have to spend your money now or the next year. Take your time and don't invest just because somebody is pushing you.

Inherited wealth

You can't choose who your parents are, but you can influence to some degree who will remember you in his last will. The odds are very small that some millionaire would give his money to someone else than his children, but it has happened in the past. As you don't know when the millionaire will die and if he will remember you in his testament, this approach is similar to gambling. A better approach is to use your millionaire friend as a bank – if you have a good business plan, you may persuade him to invest in your idea. If you know what you are doing, you will make both of you richer. If not, you will probably lose a friend.

Inheriting wealth is neither bad nor good in my opinion. The benefits are that you have big starting capital, you usually have a network of rich connections created by your parents and you can take more risks because you don't have to invest everything you have. You can keep some reserves for the bad times. Inheriting wealth can be negative if your parents haven't given you enough space to get painful experience of being without money. Also if you feel all the time, that if anything goes wrong your parents will come to the rescue, it will not help you to mature and take care of yourself on your own. Experience of being self-reliant is necessary for your self-esteem and your personal growth. Painful, character-building experience is necessary for your growth. You need to experience bad times to get used to and adapted them. Surviving bad times will make you stronger.

Inheriting wealth with responsible coaching from self-made rich parents is the best way to get rich in my opinion. What's essential is that your rich parents let you experience bad times, let you get hurt for a while and thus you become more experienced and stronger. Your character is more important than your capital in the long term. If you lose your capital, but don't know how to create it again, you will be in trouble. If I had to choose between inheriting no wealth and having space to grow my character over inheriting capital and having no space to grow and learn how to create it, I would chose to be born as a poor person. We all are born naked with zero in our bank account. It is normal to start from zero.

Being born poor and having strong survival instincts will put you on your way up. If you manage to change your status from poor to financially comfortable, you have the character needed to change from financially comfortable to rich person. You can create habit of striving for a better life, working hard and smart to get higher and higher on the social ladder.

If you are born to a financially comfortable family and you will not experience lack of money, there is a high probability that you will not have desire and ambition to get rich. You have had no reason to develop desire for something which you already have. People realize how important something is usually only after they lose it. If you were born rich or comfortable and your parents 'walked the way for you' already, it is good to step out of your comfort zone to shape your character. You can take the challenge to start your wealth without the money or connections of your parents. Experience both bad and good times and learn how to build your wealth from scratch without the help of your family.

Then get back to your family wealth with your

experience, self-esteem and knowledge and increase the family wealth. You should do it if you want to prove to yourself that you could do it even if you were not born rich. If you already are rich, you have to focus on how to stay rich and grow your wealth at the same time. Spend your time in discussion with your parents and your rich self-made friends about these topics to learn more and get new ideas how to earn more while evading predatory taxes, costs and bad investments.

Marry a millionaire

Although in the last few generations the idea or marring for money is not popular, it was considered normal in the past. Throughout history, marriages were made for strategic alliances, economic gain and other unromantic reasons. Women need support while they are pregnant and that's why they look for a partner, who will financially take care of them. We don't have to like it, but it is natural. In the same way, older men are looking for a younger, healthy woman who can get pregnant easily and is suitable to raise their children. If everything goes as they wish, there is no problem – the woman is getting her financial security in exchange for taking care of children. The problem is when man gets broke or the woman loses her ability to give birth and raise children. That pair is for fair weather only: when times are bad, they split. Marriage is a great commitment and promise to stay together even if times are bad. Think twice before you chose this way to become rich.

Illegal or immoral ways to get money – the quickest way

I don't advise you to do any illegal activities. It is however necessary to mention this way of getting rich because this way to wealth is missing in all personal development get rich books. There are many examples of people getting rich based on deception, manipulation and lies. Just read the newspapers or study the history. The risks with illegal activities are very high and it is smarter to use a legal approach if you do not have a social network which will protect you. If you decide that this is the way for you, you should act in a big way and earn millions to be able to pay the best lawyers and bribe judges, police and politicians who make laws or who can give you amnesty. Smart criminals use other people to do the dirty work and they manage their dirty business from behind the scenes.

If you are just a street thief, there is big chance you will get caught and end up in prison sooner or later. Consider getting diplomatic or other legal immunity. I hear that you can buy diplomatic attaché status with some small countries. Once you earn enough money from illegal activities, legalize it, invest it and become a rich legal investor. But to quit on illegal activities you start doing and change to law abiding citizen is easier said than done. Usually it is a one way ticket.

My aunt's husband came to Slovakia from Ukraine because he had problems with his previous gang there. He is a very well build and powerful man. From what he told me, he wanted to quit on illegal activities with his gang, but they refused to let him go.

They caught him and cut him deep into his chest, where he now has big scars. He is an easy going and thorough man. That is the reason he left Ukraine and lived in Slovakia even without a visa for a few years.

After some time I heard he had financial problems and later I heard that he got to prison because he was caught with narcotics. I believe that, once you taste the easy money, it is hard to stop and never come back to the easy money even if you want to. If you decide you have enough and want to start legal activities, your 'friends' who took part in the illegal activities can be against this, as you know too much about them. Illegal activities are a one-way ticket in my opinion. Don't start any business with dangerous people, it is not worth it. They will use you and throw you overboard if it suits them.

Stories about loyalty in gangs are not true anymore. Even if you have not been convicted of any crime, people around will know how you acquired your money and your bad reputation will be with you for the rest of your life. One way out is to leave your country and start a new life in one at the other end of world. Some gangsters made it this way and are 'good' businessmen and citizens of Central or South American countries. You can move to a different town, if nobody wants you dead, and start again. But you will have to leave your 'friends' behind. And most important, they will have to be willing to let you go.

If you are not prepared to disappear and leave your life behind, don't do it. The life of a gangster is usually rich, but it is a short life. There is a high probability that your former partners will assassinate you before you are able to disappear and start a new life abroad. I advise you not to do it, the risks are too high and risking your life and health is not worth all the money in the world. It is stupid to be the richest man in the graveyard.

Get a high paying job

A high paying job is for people who prefer a safer and slower way to get rich over freedom and adventure. There is nothing wrong with that approach and many people have done it this way before. First plan your career. Getting a high paying job usually takes a few years to build up on the experience and skills necessary for getting that high paying job. Benefits of this approach are low risk, less stress and smaller responsibilities. Cons are that you will have to work for someone else and conform with his idea of how to do your work.

Another 'con' is that if you are employed and work only from nine till five, you will have more free time and money, which usually result in spending more money on things you don't need instead of investing them. You can have a good life with less stress if you choose this way instead of running your own business. Or you can be employed during the day and work on your business during the evenings.

What you have to realize is that you may not be able to work all your life and as you grow too old to work, you simply will not be able to work anymore. In the past, people solved this by having many children who took care of their parents when they were old. Today it does not work that well. People save in their retirement plans and hope they will be paid when they retire. As banks and governments get more and more corrupt, I would not trust them to take care of me. Once you give them your money, you have none or limited control how they handle it and you have no guarantee that in crisis your money won't be taken from you by the government as it was done on Cyprus in 2013.

It is safer to invest your surplus money into assets and over your productive life period buy or create enough assets to take care of you when you can't work anymore. This process can take ten or thirty years, so don't expect to get rich fast. Take your time to analyze your future assets and don't buy them just because somebody told you to do it. Assets are items, which put money into your personal wallet. Compare how much you pay for the item and how much you receive from it. If this item gives not a positive cash flow, it is not asset but a liability.

You don't have to have a regular job. You can become a sportsman, an actor, a singer etc. What you need, is to be either top performer, who gets paid huge amounts of money for his results or to be well known and attractive for advertising. A con of being sportsman, actor or singer is that the competition is hard and most of sportsmen will not make it to the top.

Business owner

Building your own business is probably the hardest way to get rich and that is why many people don't do it, or do it and fail. Cons of building your own "money making machine" is that when you haven't tried it before, you will probably fail and lose your money and energy. If you learn from that experience, you will at least not lose your time that was spent on building your first business. You can use that experience to start your second business.

Next con which most of your employees will not understand is that you are "married" to your business and for a businessman there is nothing but work from nine till five. You will have 24 hours responsibility, you will have to get the work done by yourself if your employees quit or are on a sick leave. There is high probability that you will end with less money after a year than if you had not started your own business. That is why a safe solution is to start your business part-time at the same time with your day job. This is the path I recommend – full-time job and part-time business.

Pros of running your own business are invaluable - you will get lots of knowledge and experience and you will learn more about yourself. You will have more freedom if successful and potential financial profit is higher than when staying in a job. When you work for someone else, once you stop working (due to accident or illness) your income gets lower or stops. You are limited in your job as you can't copy yourself and have three or four full-time jobs. If your business is working for you as it should, you don't have to work anymore.

Two ways how to minimize your loss in your own business is to use a franchise model, where you will pay for proven business system or to use multi-level marketing company. We will cover building your own business in more detail later.

If you don't have big capital to invest and you do not have great idea that can be transformed into intellectual property asset, doing business can be the fastest way to get rich. It is also most difficult way for most of people if you are not natural born talent for doing business and it is not in your blood. If it is in your blood, it will be easier.

What really helps is when your parents are doing business too, because you probably learned the right attitude toward business from them. If you want to be an entrepreneur and build your business from scratch, you have to know the basics of every business aspect. When your company is profitable, while you will know only the basics of its operations, it will be even more profitable when operated by experts.

Why is starting a business so hard? You will have multiple jobs in the beginning. You will have to become a sales person, learn to say no to deals that are not profitable for you and learn how to ask for more, and you have to become your own manager and manager of other people. You have to make goals to plan your cash flow and place your expenditures in a time frame according to planned income, etc.

Starting a part-time business at home allows you to get experience in practical business skills, which are usually missing in academic learning process:

- Sales skills
- Negotiation and deal making skills
- Management skills
- Cash management skills
- Practical tax and business law basics
- Basics of accounting
- Pressure handling experience

People who have finished business school have an advantage in the first six skills. Handling pressure can be learned only by experience, and pressure that is too high is very often the reason why a person quits their own business. Being under high pressure allows you to learn more about yourself. You can find out that your bad feelings caused by the stress running a business is not enough to cover the benefits of running a business. There will be nobody you can ask what to do or to give responsibility to. This is probably the most difficult part for former employees. Complete freedom and complete responsibility.

When you decide to start a business, prepare yourself that your loved ones will try to persuade you not to do it by giving you a list of reasons why it will not work. Be prepared for hard criticism. They don't do it because they want to destroy your dream, but because they want to protect you from failure. And they usually want you to have secure income.

Sportsmen are in a very good psychological and emotional position to start a business. They are trained to work hard; they usually take a simple approach to planning and doing, are used to winning, and handle the pressure of loss. Usually when they fail, it gives them energy to fight back and work harder next time.

Sales and marketing skills

You do not have to be the first business in your industry to be successful. Most people are afraid of competition and they start business in an industry where there is no competition. This usually leads to the start of a "great" monopoly where there are no customers actually. Creating a new market takes time and lot of money. Do not be afraid of competition. If they can do it profitably, you can do it. Of course you have to do your homework first and calculate if you really will be profitable. If it is not profitable even on paper, you will not be profitable in reality. Usually your costs will be 30 % higher than your worst case budget as there will be some costs you did not include in your estimation and your sales will be 30 % lower. And your time schedule will be few weeks to months behind because of not fulfilled promises of your suppliers. Welcome to real life!

When starting a business or when you invest, you will have to learn how to sell. Be careful in thinking that potential customers will like to buy what you personally like to buy or what your potential customers said they would like to buy. Don't trust various professional polls that tell what potential customers would like to buy. People in polls tell/write down what they think you want them to tell/write down most of time. Even if they think they would like to buy something you offer, when the time for purchase comes, they won't. Why? Because it costs them nothing to state in the poll that they will buy, but the actual payment costs them some pain.

This is why you should sell what is proven that people really do buy. Not just what they would like to buy when you ask them, but what they actually already bought. For example what they already bought from your competition. Purchase that data from your competitor's employees. With marketing and sales skills you can persuade potential customers that what you are selling is exactly what they want to buy. An easier way is to look to the past and see what has been really sold. Then you can prepare your products based on past data. That's the surest way how to sell, by simply looking at what has been sold so far.

Marketing can be very expensive if you allow your employees to make it expensive. It is easier for them to throw out money and pray it will bring higher sales then to sell themselves. And don't forget that there is risk of mentioned "kickback" when they pay for advertising with your money.

When you start selling a product that has not been sold so far, you have to test the sales. Set a period of time for testing, take notes of your marketing activities, measure the sales, and then make decision if it is worth it to continue.

The marketing. Correct marketing is not about having shiny website or a nice business card. Marketing can be based on word of mouth too. Wrong marketing is expensive. You have to measure response from your marketing activities and if they don't bring profitable revenues, stop it and find other marketing activities that will bring you profits. I will repeat myself, because this is what many marketers do wrong – marketing is not about having a known brand that you can be proud of, and successful marketing is not measured by recognition percentage of your brand in some poll. Successful marketing is measured by profitable sales brought to the bank account of your company.

For example, you can take a look at Ferrari vs.

Toyota. If you will make a poll, more people would like to have the Ferrari and we can agree the Ferrari brand is much more recognized than Toyota. However, statistics show us that Toyota sells more cars with higher total profit than Ferrari. In a poll question, *"What car would you purchase if you were purchasing a car?"*, the same person who would check Ferrari instead of, e.g. Toyota, can go the next day and purchase the Toyota. Polls are not that important. The SALES and the money coming to your account are important. Good marketing is about sales, not branding. Brand is important of course, but if you have to decide if you will spend your money on activities that increase the prestige of your brand or activity that will increase your sales, which would you chose?

You can do branding for free and pay only for advertisements which bring sales.

Important activities connected with marketing and sales are testing and measurement. You have to measure costs and results of your marketing and sales activities to know which are bringing you cash and profits and which are not. Branding activities are sometimes the usual money eater with no significant impact on increased sales. Marketers like branding and creativity. It is cool to win awards for creativity, but this is not what you need. What you need is profitable sales. The only way how to know if you have profitable sales is to measure them and measure cost spent on activities leading to sales.

Always find ways to keep marketing costs low and increase profits. Profits can be increased by a) optimization of conversion rate with your current marketing activities, b) increasing sale amount by using up sales and cross sales, c) increasing repetitive purchasing by your customer, d) increasing price by increasing perceived product value by the customer or at least find ways to keep your prices adding the low-cost or no-cost extras and any kind of free gift. e) decreasing costs by their optimization.

Training rejection by dating women

One of the sales skills you need to practice is to learn how to accept and handle rejection and adversity without bad feelings. It is a natural part of living. Get used to it.

If you don't want to test on your potential customers, there is a way to learn to handle rejection is by asking unknown women for a date. You will learn how to handle rejection and you will learn more about women. This is a good example of reaching more goals with one activity. Always use those opportunities to do more tasks at the same time. Life is short, use your time well.

One of my friend's friends named Julo asked me how to approach a potential girlfriend. I said, "It is simple. You will go to a disco and ask girl for a dance. She will refuse, so you will ask another and she will refuse too. Then you will try another and another until you try it at least ten times." Julo asked "And then ... will the tenth agree to dance with me?" I quickly replied "No. But you will get used to it."

Actually dating is little more complicated, but basically it is as I wrote. If you want to learn more about proven formulas how to successfully date women, ask my publisher to push me to write a manual on how to date women.

Negotiation and deal making skills

There are many good books on negotiation and deal making. You should read some, but you also have to experience the negotiation process personally. We will cover just the basics. Try to understand your partner and try to find win-win deals. If the deal is not good for you, let it be. You don't have to make a deal with every partner. Have a set of rules to guide you towards a good deal. Never accept the deal immediately without having the option to think it through and change or cancel the deal. You can always say that you have to consult the terms of the deal with your other partner.

If you don't have the power to make your partner fulfill his part of the deal, you take the risk that he will not do it. Put your conditions of terminating the deal if it is not profitable for you into the contract. Get the best possible conditions for you and don't pity your partner.

Taxes can cost you a lot. In my second business I wanted to do everything by the book and I ended up paying 3x more in taxes than what I have earned. Tax optimization is crucial. Taxed money is money thrown into a black hole of corruption and, by paying more than you have to, you are helping the crime connected to the government to thrive. Protect your business from taxes or you may end up bankrupt. Even great companies like Google are optimizing taxes and move cash offshore to evade predatory taxation. It is always better to invest the money than have it taxed. Many companies choose to have cash over showing profit in accounting. They even show loss and ask government for subsidies to create or to keep the jobs. You can be profitable and still go bankrupt, because your customers will not pay you on time and your sales (which are taxed) will not transform to cash on your bank account.

You are dealing with people when doing business and real business is far from what you learned about business in school. Promises and deals are not fulfilled always as they should be, or not at all. You can go to the court for a lawsuit, but let's be realistic, your righteous claims enforcement by court is long, costly and, in the end, usually not profitable. Think then about a lawsuit with not an American, but a Chinese company. You would have to be a really big corporation to get results in the foreign court. The only person who will get rich on your lawsuit will be your lawyer. Lawsuits are not good for business. Remember, if you have a good deal, you have a promise that the other part of the deal will do what they agreed on. Do not consider the promise to be fulfilled automatically. Expect that people do not keep their promises – usually people who are in business are flexible with their promises (they could get angry if we use the word liar, they like being called a flexible person much, much more). It is not right, but we are not in an ideal world and not everyone is able to keep their word. Not everyone who breaks their promise does this because they want to. They sometimes really want to keep the agreement, but it is not possible for them at that particular time.

You will learn how to handle pressure only by being under pressure. Do research and find out what is the worst that can happen to you in your situation. This will allow you to see the facts and can lower your fear and the pressure. If you are not going to jail or nobody wants to kill you, it is not such a big deal as you may think. When you would like to start a new business, but you don't know which to choose, ask yourself, "How can I change problems and something negative into business opportunities?" Where are problems, there are the opportunities. Where are opportunities, there is money. This is the hardest way with the possible highest profits.

It would be Easier to look around you and search for businessmen that are rich, and start the same business as they do. You don't have to start doing something that nobody else is doing. You can copy someone's business if it is not intellectual property. Look for opportunities how can you do the same as they do, but faster, more convenient for the customer, with added value, with better service, etc. Look at telecommunication, software and internet companies as generally the best choice.

Or you can find a suitable franchise for yourself and pay for the system already created.

Management skills

In business you have to manage yourself and also your employees or suppliers. Spend your time on planning and management. Don't just work, work, and work on every task that needs to be done. There is so much that needs to be done, that one person can't do it all by himself. Divide tasks according to priority and deadlines. Erase tasks that are time consuming and bring low or no profit. Spend time on thinking and learning how can you make your business more profitable.

You, as a business owner, have to focus on your primary task – creating a system for your company that gets sustainable results even if you are not working for your company yourself. Ask yourself – How can your company work without your interference? Can you copy your company system a hundred times to new companies without you being there?

Cash flow management skills

Cash flow is the blood of your business. Ask for an advance payment or for a deposit from your future customer, if possible. Pay your supplier after you have the money from your customer. These options are based on your negotiation skills, because most customers and suppliers will refuse to do that with a new company. Try to find someone reputable to make a guarantee for you. Of course you should refuse credits to your new customers and should ask your supplier for extended credit. Just be realistic and expect they will refuse. It sounds so nice and easy in all those cash flow advices and tips, but it is not that easy in reality in all the markets. Always add "Late payments can be penalized with xx% for each day of late payment." Using "can" is better than "will", because it leaves you space for negotiation and if you are willing to solve the payment problem with your customer, you are not obliged to demand the percentage from customer.

Good customers are important. Bad customers should be sent to your competition. Remember that a customer is someone who pays for your services. If he does not pay, he is still a prospect, not a customer.

Have some reserves for unexpected problems. For example, I paid a 30% deposit to our Chinese supplier to produce pillows for us and deliver them in January. However, because of his problems, the pillows were delivered 6 months later. By the time we received them, the product life cycle of the pillows was at the end. This can happen. When budgeting, I recommend that you to overestimate expenses and underestimate revenues.

When planning cash flow, always underestimate sales and overestimate costs. A good rule of thumb is to use 30% for both underestimates and overestimates. When your business looks profitable even after this change, you will be better off if something unexpected happens. Most of the companies use debt for their growth financing. When you grow, expect that when your revenues grow arithmetically, your costs will grow exponentially.

Investor/Trader

If you want to get rich by investing or trading, you have to have control over money or over something of value. You can even invest money that you don't own. You can trade or barter items which you don't own and charge fees for your service. Chances that you will raise capital needed to trade profitably are small. The usual situation is that you will have to invest your own money, which you earned and saved in your job, business, etc. Investing in assets is crucial for your wealth plan and more detail about investing and trading will be covered later. Trading is considered more professional than a source of passive income, because without your work you will not receive additional cash. A popular option is automatic trading – a computer program will do all the trading for you.

An investor himself is the most important asset. It is him who can change property into an asset or into a liability. Without him, there will be no one to obtain and manage assets. It is you, the investor, who will analyze investment options. It is you who has to decide if the partners for the investment are the right one, or if they will cheat you. It is you who has to do corrective measures when something goes wrong and asset costs you more than they earn. Good investors can change bad investments into good ones. With good due diligence, an investor can separate opinions from facts.

Work hard on yourself; it is you who makes the difference. By becoming a good investor you start to attract good deals. First think of whom you have to become to get what you want. You can invest for capital gain or for cash flow. With capital gains you risk more for potential higher profits. With cash flow your risks are smaller, but also profits are lower.

Most millionaires got rich by capital gain. Some did it through creating a company and then selling shares of it. Others did it by purchasing goods cheap and selling them high with a nice profit.

Generally recommended rules for investors and businessmen are:

1. Be a person of integrity and be truthful at least to yourself. Don't lie to yourself. See the facts as they are. Understand the risks and take protective measures if necessary. (*I saw many opportunists to be better off financially without having any signs of integral behavior.*)

2. Keep your eyes open and your mind open for changes and opportunities. See things as they could be, not only as they are now. Search with your mind, not only with your eyes.

3. Use modern technology to find, analyze, obtain and control assets. We are in a global world so think globally. The biggest opportunities can be found where the biggest problems are.

4. Understand financial statements; see the story behind the historical numbers.

5. Understand people's motives and watch out for liars.

6. Start with an exit strategy – know how to protect your money and assets. Plan your cash flow, income, spending and taxes.

I found out that there are mostly two types of businessman – 1. **Simple approach people** who act based on a simple plan and, 2. **Complicated approach people** who act only after they have thoroughly planned their actions and take into consideration all aspects and problems that can occur. The biggest problem with the 2nd group is that they lose time and, because they understand the risks, they do not start to act. This second group is better suited for an employee's position. The employees are often rewarded for not making mistakes, while entrepreneurs or sales people are rewarded for results.

The first group usually starts with a basic plan and then they figure out how to solve problems when they occur. They tend to bend the rules and some do not keep their promises if it does not suit them. The first group does not fear the consequences of their actions. The second group understands the risks and consequences if something goes wrong and usually they do not risk.

There is equation – The more you know, the bolder you have to be to take action.

If you are not a very bold person, you have to 1. Become more primitive to simplify your plan and action or 2. Become bolder. It would be best to become more primitive and more bold at the same time. Simple people tend to have happier life. Too complicated people tend to "create" problems where they are not, or where they are not yet. A simple person solves the problem after it becomes a problem. He is not going to waste his energy on something that probably will never happen. A complicated person wants to prevent a problem from happening and he spends his energy to "solve" problems, which do not yet exist.

Real estate investor

Even real estate investing is not the bulletproof way how to get rich. However, it is one of the most probable ways. The second after having your own business. For real estate investing you will need money supply your business should provide. So far the best option I could find is to start with a business and use that money to secure your position by purchasing and renting real estate. Don't invest in old money like gold and silver or new money like bitcoin or litecoin for security. You can trade precious metals and new currencies, but if it is not bringing you money each month, it is trading and not investing. It is better to create a business around precious metals and currencies and be paid small commission on each transaction. Let others keep the risks of trading and keep your secure commission.

The benefit of purchasing, renting and selling real estate is that it does not take much time. You can keep your day job or run your business and still invest in real estate. You have risk is in every investment - even if you put your money in a bank account (as we saw in Cyprus case, where 60% of deposits were stolen from the bank customers by the government and banks). You are paid interest rate on a bank account. While there is chance that your bank will go bankrupt, the chance of that happening and not being paid your money is very small. The same goes for real estate.

If you choose the right location and negotiate profitable conditions for mortgage, purchasing, renting, and taking care of the property, you can make stable profitable cash flow. There is always risk that rental prices will drop in the market, you will have to lower your income, and your assets become a liability. If you keep a significant profit rate when you purchase the property, you have space to keep your estate in assets column. It is difficult to find a good deal, but you have enough time to invest, you don't have to buy your first property tomorrow. Deal negotiation is crucial. If someone is desperate to sell, you can find a very good deal. Old people or people who need money quickly can be desperate and good partners for your first property. Another way to get good deals is to see changes that will increase rental value of that property.

Real estate investments are long-term investments and before purchasing one you have to be sure of your calculations. If the numbers don't work, don't buy it even if you like it. Real estate properties usually are not sold overnight, so take your time to think about it. Investing in real estate is suitable for patient people.

Intellectual property owner

Intellectual property is the legal expression for exclusive rights toward intangible property. Legal vehicles protecting that property are copyrights, trademarks, patents, and industrial design rights. Common properties are musical, literary, artistic works; discoveries and inventions; business processes which are expressed through words, phrases, symbols, and designs. If you own or control intellectual property and nobody is paying money for it, it is not an asset. You can either sell the property (brand, database, software, know how, book etc.) or you can receive royalties.

Protection of intellectual property (IP) is critical to prevent others from using it without your permission. Laws for intellectual property protection were created to "promote progress" as to give inventors and creators incentive to invent and create property which will be beneficial for the society. With exclusive rights, owners of IP can achieve financial benefits by using or allowing others to use their IP. A great benefit of IP is that you have to create it only once. If you have a contract with someone else to sell it for you, it becomes a real passive asset. You will just collect the money and pay your taxes.

All you have to remember about intellectual property is that you have to protect it legally with copyrights, trademarks, patents, and industrial design rights once you create them. Purchasing intellectual property from someone else will be profitable only when your business needs it or if its seller is desperate and sells below its real price.

Paper assets owner

Paper assets are the easiest assets to get in and to get out. This is why they are so popular. Common paper assets are stocks, bonds, mutual funds, term accounts, or documents with rights for commodities. You can invest for cash flow or for capital gains. Big money is earned by investing for capital gains, but this is also riskier as you can't know what the price of your investment paper asset will be in the future when you plan to sell it. If you really want to invest in paper assets and minimize risks, you have to invest with control over that paper asset. If it is stock, to get control, you have to get decision-making share in that company as Warren Buffet does or you have to be the one who creates those paper assets by bringing your company public as Mark Zuckerberg did.

Quickest way in paper assets business is to buy significant share in state owned company with a discount. With proper bribe you will get huge discount – you just need the top manager willing to publish accounting data showing the company is fit for bankruptcy and you will get the business almost for free, because you are going to "save" the company by investing in it. Real valuable assets of the company are "hidden in accounting" until you buy it. Then you transfer the really valuable assets into daughter companies you create and own and let the mother company keep all the bad debts and unprofitable business operations. Then you will make few contracts between mother and daughter companies which are very good for daughter companies and not so good for the mother company. And then all you have to do is to have the state top manager to announce that the mother company is in very good shape and the state is buying back your share. They will pay you huge amount of money plus you will be given 100% share in the daughter companies as a compensation for making the mother company profitable again. That's all. You are done. All you have to do now is to pick nice (and expensive of course) house near the sea and enjoy your life, because you can retire now.

Except for Foreign Exchange trading, mutual funds, and term accounts, I do not have much experience with paper assets. After trying Forex, it looks to me more like horse bets. With computer trading and manipulation by big players, markets do not act based on fundamental expectations. Mutual funds and term accounts are very safe investment vehicles, but they are also with small or negative profits. If you run your own business, you will have higher interest rates when you use your money in your business. With business you have much higher control and leverage. If you trade paper assets for capital gain or cash flow, I recommend you to do it through legal entity – your company for tax optimization.

Know yourself

Who you are determinates what your life will look like. If you behave like a rich person, you will become rich. Getting and staying rich is not about luck. It is about how you think and what you do. Who you are is based on your nature and your experience. Rich people do things that others are too lazy or afraid to do. You can quickly change your character and values if you face extreme situations and break your ego or self-pity. I know it is hard to change yourself and most people will not change much during their lifetimes. But changing your character is possible if you are willing to pay the price. You can change yourself also by changing your habits, by changing your thinking, by changing what you study, by changing your words and by changing your actions.

What you study is what you will become. When you study something, you start to think about that subject and use vocabulary of that subject. Then your thoughts and your words create your actions related to that subject. If you study health, you will start eating and sleeping healthier. If you study wealth, you will start to create your wealth. Also, who you spend your time with shapes your actions. Your repetitive actions become your habits. Your habits shape your character and your character shapes your future. Be selective with your thoughts, words and people you meet. They decide your future.

Before you start to shape your future, it is smart to know who you are right now and who you were. You need to know where you are now to make realistic plans for your future. Writing down your status right now will give you feedback in few years when you look back at the path you made. This part of book will help you to understand where you stand right now. It might not be a pleasant view, but it is necessary to be honest with yourself and write down just the facts. Don't describe your situation as better than it is in reality. Don't describe it as worse than it is in reality. Stick to the facts. After a year, do the same task and then you will see the real path that you have made over a one year period. One year may seem like very long time to you now, but if you will be active and use that time to your maximum, it will pass quickly. With this feedback you will see if you are going the right or wrong direction towards your goals. It will give you better overall perspective of your life.

Having a plan for reaching your future goals is essential if you want to be sure to reach them. You may succeed without the plan, but the only bulletproof way to success is to plan. Divide your plan into years, months, weeks and days. Tasks of your daily to do list should be partial goals of your weekly and monthly goals. Monthly goals should be part of your year goals.

The only way to influence your future is by doing something right NOW. The past is gone, the future is yet to come. Don't postpone important goals all the time. NOW is the right time to start. When you finish reading this book and you will not have a written plan on how you want to find out your purpose in life within a week, you can stop reading this book right now. You have to do something to get results. Making a plan is the smallest step you can do. If you have no idea what could be your purpose, you can start by looking at the zodiac and searching what are recommended work positions for you.

How can a family ruin your life and your success. Even if they love you.

Do not show your personal plans to anyone if possible. Most important, don't show it to your family or your friends if you are not 100% sure, they will support you. Although they love you and they are willing to help, it is proven to do more damage than good to consult your character plans with them. Keep it under your hat. They do want your best and they will try to keep you in your and their comfort zone. They consider it safe and smart. They don't want to see you get hurt. They will prevent you from getting hurt. And out of your comfort zone you will get hurt in the beginning. It is natural process of learning the important stuff - by trial and error. That is the way you learned to walk, remember. You fell and got hurt. And then you stood up and walked.

If people who you are going to show your plans are not successful themselves in your opinion, their advice is not qualified and can do damage to you even if given with best intention. Consult them only if you consider them significantly more successful than you already are right now.

Why NOT to retire

Have you seen what happens to retired people who just sit idle at home and do not want to have any problems? Not even a garden, a dog or chess? How depressed end up women at home if their kids grow up and they suddenly have no one to take care of? How employees rot alive if they just sit and get bored without any problems to solve? They are dying while they are still alive.

Principle of happiness and the meaning of your life

If you are looking for happiness look at the children. If there is still some child left in you, you know everything about the happiness subject. Small kids create some task for them each day and then solve that "problem". To build a sand castle with towers, to build up a tower made of cubes, to exchange balls for a knife or to draw a picture of the sun. They are trying, make effort, labor hard. With great enthusiasm they go through the barriers and follow their goal.

They are not afraid of barriers and problems, they simply overcome them. Their sole existence, their work and action has a meaning and results. What they do we call a game, but that is life - a game.

When they play they do not have time to be hungry, thirsty or unhappy, because they have their problem to solve. They are happy. Their energy and power is used to reach for them important goals and they have the feeling, that their life has a meaning.

What is your meaning of life? Is it to take care of your family? Is it to create something that will be remembered for centuries? Is it to help other people live their lives better? Is it to conquer all your fears and thus become a truly free man? Is it to find your passion and your love and serve them well?

All you need to be happy is to have a goal (or a problem to solve) each day and solve it by the end of the day. You will be satisfied and happy. This problem solving will make you wake up early and feel great in the evening. Spending your time with problem solving and finding a solution is the road to happiness. The problem can be e.g. to prepare breakfast for your children, take them to school, spend your time at work, prepare dinner for the family and to check what was the day of your family like in the evening. If that is your goal and you finish it by the night, you have done a great job and can go to bed with a satisfactory and happy smile.

Find a quiet place, take your time and think about yourself. Write down who you think you are and what is important for you. Describe your character in writing not just by thinking or talking. It is O.K. to rewrite and rewrite until you are positive that what you have written down is the real you. Write down not what you wish to be, but what you honestly believe you are at this period of your life. What you wish to be will be written later.

To have your own "good" problem and to overcome it daily – this is the principle of happiness. Do you know people who don't have any problems? Their approach is: I just do not want to have any problems. Leave me alone.

But life does not work that way ... only the dead do not have any problems.

If you will not establish and start solving a goal for yourself (increase sales, build a house, learn foreign language, take care of your family ...), the LIFE will make create a problem somehow for you. Or someone else will throw his problem at you. And he will not ask you if you like it or not.

We always have problems, but it is a difference what kind of problems do we have.

Who am I?

My strengths	My weaknesses

Example of your today's strengths and weaknesses

My strengths	My weaknesses
I am healthy, strong and full of energy I experienced loosing lot of money and managed to handle it both emotionally and financially I was misused by liars and manipulators and I know how to spot them now before I make business with them	I am stubborn I still need more experience with handling fear or rejection I need to conquer my laziness every day ...

I am disciplined and I do what needs to be done when necessary even if I don't feel like doing it	
I quickly adapt to the situation and people around me	
I am a quick learner and I efficient worker	
I am goal oriented and dedicated	
I am willing to spend my free time on personal development	
I am no longer shy	
When I start something, I finish it	
I am a man of honor and I keep my word	
I am financially secure	
I am not afraid to get in the way of bullies	
I am ready to learn from any obstacle which life will put in front of me to teach me a lesson	
I am impatient, which allows	

me to do more in less time ...	

For orientation in which direction your life goes write what strengths and weaknesses you had ten or twenty years ago.

My strengths were	**My weaknesses were**

Example of past strengths and weaknesses

My strengths were	**My weaknesses were**
I was a quick learner and studied hard	Lack of self-esteem and self-respect
I dreamed of being a	Lack of strength and courage

powerful man When pushed into a corner, I fought back ...	Pessimist, shy and introverted person I was being bullied around Depressive thoughts ... Simply said, I was loser

Everybody has strengths and weaknesses. And if you could not think of any of your strengths, write down at least "I am willing to study success". You read this book and that means you are willing to spend your time studying and separate yourself from losers who don't care about their future or are too lazy to do something about it. You have made the first step towards a better future – you started to study what you wish to be or to have. Remember that what you study and do is what you become. If you study wealth and act like a wealthy person, you will become one.

Look down at your strengths and weaknesses list. Are you satisfied with who you are now? Do you see positive progress from who you were in your past?

If yes, that is great. If not, you should change something in your plan.

Let us look on character of successful people. Definition of success is subjective to each person. One of my favorite definitions is: '**To get up in the morning, go to bed in the evening and be able to do what you love in-between.**'

There are more definitions on successful

people. Common ground among them is having enough money and time to do what you want to do. If you look at bank robbers, they have enough money to do what they want to do, but only until they are caught. Are they good example of successful people? I don't think so, because their way of life is not sustainable, they will get caught over time and in jail they will not be able to do what they wish to do during the day.

What about politicians? They are famous, have power and have money. Are they successful? Would you like to be a politician?

The life of politician is not suitable for everyone. They very often make and break deals and they have to make public statements according to their sponsor's wishes. Not every politician does that, but I believe most of them do. From what I saw they are just very good paid employees of oligarchs. They usually get rich by dividing government money to their 'business partners' and taking part of it. And most of people are afraid of public speaking, which is a must for a politician. For most people politician is much more difficult job than anything else, including cleaning toilets.

We will probably agree that sportsmen, actors and singers are successful if they are world famous and rich, right? Would you like to be one? Do you have necessary physical or mental prepositions as they do? Are you willing to make the huge sacrifices they had to?

The average person will answer yes; he will make the sacrifices and do everything necessary. But the average person will not really do what he says he will. Average person does not have the extraordinary discipline world class sportsmen, singers or actors have to have. Even if the average Joe starts, he will not sustain all the years of hard work with small hope to reach what top performers did. To be world champion, you have to be better than thousands or millions of others. Competition is high, and the chance of success is small. The process of getting to the top is painful. You will get hurt. Everybody does. What makes the difference is your determination to reach your goal and what are you willing to sacrifice to reach it. Do you really want this? Are you willing to pay the price?

If your answer is yes, read biographies of people you admire. Project a role model and ask yourself what would he do right now. What are the values, qualities and attributes of successful people that you most admire? Write down strengths and weaknesses of a person you would like to be in the future.

Common among successful people is to be impatient, humble, persistent, truthful, active, stubborn, goal oriented. Many successful people who run their own businesses worked 20 years until they became rich; they wake up at 5:00 and go to bed at 23:00.

Ask yourself: Who is the person who will get everything you desire? Do you want to be that person?

Look at Will Smith. He says that he is successful because he still works while other guys sleep or eat. In his first episodes of Fresh Prince he learned not just his lines, but the whole cast's; he memorized the whole script. With that kind of determination and sacrifice he is doomed for success.

Now write down what characteristics you would like to have. Focus on most important strengths and accept your weaknesses. Your weaknesses make you balanced as a human being. Once you put your weaknesses on paper, find out if they can be corrected quickly without losing focus on your strengths and then stop thinking about them very much. Focus on what you want to become, not on what you don't want to. Become the better version of yourself. Don't focus on your weaknesses and their correction. Start with your strengths and talents. For weaknesses – all you have to know is what they are and then make sure somebody else will do what you can't.

I will say it once more, because it is important and it will save you lot of time and lot of trouble. **Accept your weaknesses and focus on your strengths.**

Your future strengths and weaknesses

My strengths will be	My weaknesses will be

Example of future strengths and weaknesses

My strengths will be	My weaknesses will be
Healthy, mentally and physically strong, energetic and relaxed	Stubborn, but under control
	Impatient, but able to control it
Experienced when dealing with people and immune to manipulation	Introvert and shy person
	...

Experienced winner Disciplined Understanding and controlling my fears Adaptable and quick learner Goal oriented Financially secure, comfortable and wealthy …	

    I was an introverted and shy person, and probably, deep in my character, I still am. People don't change that much. Although I have almost no problem speaking publicly or addressing unknown attractive women, it is not completely natural to me. I just got used to it. I do not seek social events and I don't need to meet a lot of people. I was afraid to speak publicly, so I found a way where I had to speak in front of public – I started to teach at the university and now I speak in front of other people, on conferences in front of managers of big companies without a second thought when it needs to be done. I don't have to like it, but what must be done, will be done.

    If you are afraid of something, you should do it just to conquer your fears. With a little bit of experience, it will be nothing terrible to speak publicly even without preparation, if you know your subject well. By repeated public speaking you will get used to it. Soon you will understand that public speaking is like regular speaking to your friends. If you make a mistake, so what? Smile, correct yourself and continue. It is normal to make mistakes. Everybody makes mistakes and most of your audience understands it. Even the best public speakers make mistakes from time to time. They are normal people like us. You can become your own hero. It is maybe hard to imagine but even presidents or super heroes like Jet Li and Will Smith has to use the bathroom and toilet paper just like the rest of the population. Once you get to the top, stay humble, you are just a human like everybody else around you. One day you can drive Mercedes and the second week you can drive old pick-up. But the car you drive does not change your character. You will be the same person if you are rich and drive the Mercedes and the same person if you drive the pick-up. There will be highs and lows in your life – and your job is to connect the highs as close to them as possible.

If you are afraid of refusal (usually people who doubt their self-worth are afraid of it) you can practice refusal by dating girls or women – based on how old you are. Your goal is not to be refused, but to experience your reaction to refusal you receive. Study your reaction, your thoughts and your feelings. Understand that **you are not your thoughts or your reactions**. You can control your thoughts and your reactions.

If you are afraid to speak to attractive women, you should do it just for the training of overcoming that fear. When you ask them for a date and you are refused nine times before finding one that was willing to go with you, don't worry. You will find her sooner or later, you just need more experience with picking the right one and shaping your character and status to attract them.

Get used to rejection and don't take it personally if she refuses. There was nothing wrong with you; she just was not interested that particular time. Smile at her and keep your head high. She might not be interested right now, but maybe she will be interested in the future. Or she might have pretty friend who may be interested in you and that is why she refused. Behave like a gentleman and don't burn the bridge towards friendly relationship with the woman.

It happened to me, that a girl who refused to dance with me came an hour later to ask me to dance, apologizing because she could not do it earlier as she had to take care of her friends. Sometimes they wish to go with you, but they can't because of their duties. Blair Singer, in his audio book the Sales Dogs, has great ideas on how to handle rejection. I strongly recommend you to listen to it multiple times. He explains things dog simple and everybody can understand his ideas and practice them. Adversity is natural part of life and you have to learn how to handle it.

It is natural that people will not give you something you wish for each time you ask for it. But still it is better to forget your ego and keep looking for the one person that will.

Note: If you want to be more experienced and more confident with women, study dating rituals and processes. You can google for good advices or you can check our website www.preshovus.com for successful dating related manuals, We are planning to publish it soon. If the book still is not there, subscribe to the newsletter and we will inform you when it will be ready for you.

You can achieve anything you can imagine - once you will dedicate your life to it

When handling goals which are considered by others as "unrealistic", there is no place for your mindset telling you *'I will try and see if it can be done.'* You have to believe it is possible and it becomes possible. If you really want to do something, do it. Don't let anybody tell you it can't be done. History is full of examples of extraordinary things that were done even if they were labeled as impossible. Once you make a decision, make sure there is no way back. Burn the bridges which go back and you will create a situation where succeeding is your only option.

If somebody did it before you, copy his behavior and do it like he did it. If nobody did it and you think it is not realistic, ask yourself if you really want to get it and do what is necessary to get it. This could mean changing your goals, putting this one on the top and focusing all your energy on one single goal sacrificing the others until you reach your ultimate goal. Ask yourself why you want it and if you are ready to die for it. If you still want it, you will get it or you will die trying to get it. It is that simple.

Great book which will help you to find your ultimate life's purpose is <u>Good to Great by Jim Collins</u>. This book was a blessing for me. His Hedgehog concept helped me to realize what I can be the best in the world at and I believe everybody who is interested in personal development has to read this treasure house of ideas.

Sports can teach you what you are made of.

Even if you fail, you are still valuable as a human being. Every good person should understand that he is a valuable member of society and he can help and serve others. You can make the difference and make better the lives of other people. Or lives of animals if the people have disappointed you in the past. Your value is inside of you and it depends only on you if your actions will be valuable for people around you.

Don't forget that everybody makes mistakes, but instead of focusing what you did wrong, focus on what was beneficial in your actions and what you gave the society. You can't make everybody happy. If you made 95% happy, and you hear the loudest 5% which are not satisfied with you, just forget the 5%. They are not worth your attention, and don't let those 5% shift your focus from what is important – it is those 95% who were happy. If you can't ignore the 5% yet, learn how to forgive yourself for your mistakes and focus on what was a success. Usually people will be thankful to you silently and ungrateful loudly. That is how people are, accept it. The 5% will be louder than the 95%.

Self-blame still has an important place in your growth - learning something about your mistakes allows you to take corrective action. But self-blame is meant to be as short as possible. Learn what you have to quickly and throw the blame away. Do it before it hurts you. Understand what you did wrong, what could be done better and let the self-blame go away. *Are you able to let go your past failures and forgive yourself?*

Now let's get back to your past. Try to remind yourself what were you doing when you felt greatest feelings of self-esteem? Write them down, so you can remind them easier next time when you will need to boost your morale.

I felt I was very important and my self-esteem grew high when...

How can you repeat those feelings?

What are your greatest achievements that you are most proud of?

I am proud of myself for ...

    Remind yourself of your past successes. Be nice to yourself. Being nice to yourself is important when you do want to be nice to others.

Your motivation, success and failures

Find out what you most enjoy doing at work, what you find easy to learn and do. Think of your past. Start from your childhood to the present day. You can think not only of pleasant activities, but also about those unpleasant, which started burning fire in your blood when you saw them. Who would you like to be like? Who do you admire? Would you like to live life similar to theirs and do what they did? If they could do it, you can do it.

You have to find what motivates you and what are you very good at. Start by looking back to your school times and see which subjects interested you so much, that you did not have to even try to study them and you were still very good at those subjects. Then go forward in time and try to remember what activities were you willing to do for free and you had good results with them.

Your decision depends also on your current health and age. If you are still young, you can become anyone. Even the world karate champion. If you are older and there is statistically small chance that you can still become the karate champion, you can start karate world championship for seniors. Only limits you have are those, you allow in your head yourself. Anything can be achieved if you dedicate your life to that goal. Bigger goals are better. If your goal is big enough, you can get sponsors to support you.

When you know what you are really good at, you can identify your talents. Think about how to describe your talents until you are satisfied. This is not competition to see who has the best talents. Stick to the facts and write them down. Don't write down talents you wish to have, write down talents you really have. Think about your past and activities where you achieved better results than people around you.

If you still can't figure out what your talents are, it is probably because you don't know yet what you are good at. Ask your long-term friends for help. They can give you hint what they think you are really good at. If you can't describe your talents or can't find any use for it, you have to get more experience and try different activities. You have to try until you find out what useful talents you have. Maybe you need just one more skill to make your talent usable on your road to riches. Or maybe you need to hire a person with the talent you lack and make a great team. Business is a team sport.

The most important task of a man during his life is to find his life's purpose and fulfill it. It is not only about what you do, but also with whom you do it. Most happiness in life comes from relationships. People were created to give and help others. Your purpose can change during your life as you experience new situations. For example, if you are homeless, your purpose could be finding enough food, being healthy and having warm and dry place to sleep. Person who is homeless can be happy with that purpose. If you are reading this book, you are in a much better situation and your ambitions can reach much higher.

When you decide what you want to do, make everything possible within your means to be the best. Excellence will drive your motivation faster and faster. You will be burning with energy once you come to the phase where you understand that you can be the best in the world.

Wish for more problems to solve and wish for more skills

Problem solving is learning. Every problem has solution and the problem has been sent to you to teach you something. The bigger problems you solve, the bigger person you become. With each bigger problem solved, previous problems seem smaller and easier for you to solve the next time. Problems were created for you, to teach you a lesson. If the problem is too big for you at certain time, you will fail. You should look at the problem as a gift. If you understand that problem can be a hidden opportunity, it will be easier for you to solve it.

Problems work according to Murphy's law. They come at the worst possible time. Think about this for a moment. If the problem reaches you at a time when it would be very easy for you to solve it, what would you learn? Not much, because you would not have to work hard on the solution and you will not get to the edge of your limits. If you operate at the edge of your limits, you learn and grow fastest.

Be the problem solver and solution finder and your growth will be enormous. Push your limits with every problem given to you further and be a 'no-limit' person. People will pay you a lot for solving their biggest problems.

When you finish your task successfully, reward yourself and celebrate. This helps to keep you going on. Give yourself a pat on the back. Most of times there will be nobody to give you that pat on the back. And we people crave for that pat so much. How many times have you expected your boss to give you praise for a job well done and he stayed silent?

Look at sportsmen how they celebrate right after scoring a goal. Do the same, it works.

When you experience failure, never say that it is you who failed. Say you have received a feedback on your plan. It is the plan that was not successful, not you. Be grateful for feedback, as you have just learned how not to do it and you are one step closer to your success.

If you are new at e.g. shooting, it will be hard for you to hit the target with your first shot. You have to practice and expect things not to be successful in the beginning. Success will come after multiple tries, failures, errors and lessons learned. The faster you fail, the more you learn and faster become successful. It is a painful road to go, but it is the best and most proven road to success. Never give up on your dreams!

If your dream is to be wealthy and your business just went broke, take some time and think if this particular business is the right road to wealth for you and what could be done better. You will learn what works for you and what does not. Maybe you should try a different business or forget your own business at all and try investing or creating intellectual properties. You have to decide for yourself, but never give up on your real dreams. There is a way for you to reach it, for sure. If you want to be successful faster, increase the speed of your failures and learn from them.

When you only study and analyze your mistakes, what will you find out about success? Yes, you are right, you will find nothing about success, but you will find how to avoid the mistakes. That is what employees do – they work in a way which protects them from mistakes, because their goal is not to be fired.

But to find out more about success, you have to study the success. Focus on building up your strength, not on correction of your weaknesses. Failure is not the mirror image of success. Copy behavior of successful people and ask them how they did it.

Your mindset

The most important asset which can make you rich is your dedication or passion to become rich. Your passion and your dedication to do what is necessary to do will help you when the situation tries to push you down to your knees. You will be experiencing ups and downs, that's as natural as four seasons of the year. After profitable autumn there will be winters which will bring you losses, be prepared for them.

You need a really good reason to go through all the obstacles to becoming rich. If you do not have a good reason to continue, you will be stopped when obstacles emerge. You can change your approach to reach your dream, but never quit on reaching the dream. If you have to do bad things to reach the goal, do them. It is natural – look at the sportsmen like Lance Armstrong – he was doping. If you are successful and you reach your goals, people will be tolerant of your mistakes and bad behavior.

Remember that it usually is not the most intelligent or smartest person who wins. Usually it is the most determined person who will win. It is the person who is willing to go one step further than the competition. Once you reach power and success, you will have time and money to rewrite history and make yourself look better.

We, the western civilization, are losing values such as discipline or self-sacrifice. It is natural because of what we see in TV. It is corrupt politicians, top managers of corporations or 'overnight created music superstars.' These are people we see and young people want to be like them. If politicians can steal legally and never go to jail, or if music companies create new pop superstars every few weeks, why should you work hard, right?

This shift of values and morality we are experiencing is replacing our image of the successful person prototype. A smart person is no longer the one who creates or invents something, but someone who steals in a big way and with legal cover. They are the elite and the average person wants' to have what they have, to increase his own prestige. Success is not measured by what you have done or what you have become, but by what you have and how valuable items you own or control.

Items you purchase can make you temporarily happy, but things you create or accomplish will make you happy long-term. It is who you are and not what you have that defines you. Look for the great example of George Bush junior. Alcoholic became a president. But this is a normal event – Boris Yeltsin was alcoholic also, and he became president. And if alcoholics can become presidents, are there any real limits for you, except those you make yourself?

Usually it is not the smartest person that wins. With a simpler approach you can have better results because you don't waste your energy on the unimportant stuff. How you achieve the goal will be forgotten. That is why it is not that important as long as you can justify your actions. The only important thing that matters in the end is whether you reach your goal or not. And believe me, people benefiting from your riches will try hard to believe whatever you will tell them and we all know that a lie which was told ten times becomes the truth.

Everybody can reach his dreams. I mean

everybody. It does not matter if you are handicapped or not. It does not matter if you are a loser right now and it does not even matter if you believe in yourself. If you want to reach your goal and you take action, your subconscious mind will guide your actions to reach the goal. Just be specific with what exactly do you want. If you want to be rich, than having money has to be more important to you than having the truth.

What self-limiting beliefs do you have that might be holding you back? Are they real or are they a lie repeated hundreds of times? What if those things weren't true at all?

You will find more information about changing your beliefs in the chapter on brain programming.

If you want to be rich, you have to define what rich means to you. To become rich and stay rich is more about what you do with what you have, than what you have now. Everybody has some assets he can use to accumulate wealth. The average person sleeps eight hours a day. This means if you have an average sleep time, each day you wake up and you have 16 hours you can invest in activities for your get-rich plan. If you are getting a paycheck regularly, you can spend part of it on accumulation of assets. This means anybody can become rich. But if you want to get rich quickly, that is another story. You have to become elite.

How you spend your time and money decides if you are becoming rich or if you are becoming poor. Unfortunately, the middle class vanishes. In the near future you will be shifted towards either the rich side or the poor side of the population. There will be just the rich and the economic slaves paying their debts off.

Think long-term

If you get rich in five years, you have done it quickly compared to others. Most people get rich in ten and more years. Most people become millionaires after they are fifty years old. Think long-term and plan your five-year get-rich plan into years, then months, weeks and days. This will keep you on the right track. If you are dedicated and talented, you can become rich in few months. Your life is more than statistics and averages.

Stop complaining

Accept full responsibility for your life. You are the one in full control of your life. You are the only one who can change your life for the better. You can ask others to help you, but you are still the only one responsible. If you are a businessman, don't complain about the crisis, market situation, about the suppliers, employees or customers.

If you don't have everything you need to reach your goal yourself, cooperate with other people. Let them do the work you can't. You have to work with what you have and stop complaining about that you don't have perfect conditions under which to operate. There is no such a thing as having the perfect conditions to start. Obstacles are natural. Don't wish for fewer problems, wish for more skills.

The obstacles and problems are actually good for you because they limit your competition and make you stronger. Search for answers how others did what you want to achieve. If they had a better starting position than you had, so what? It will take you longer time to get there, but it is still possible for you to get there. You just have to pay the price – which can be your time, your energy or your money. Or you can pay with your health and your life if you want to reach a goal that is bigger than your life.

If you can change the situation to suit you more, do it. If you can't, then accept it. It would be nice to have two springs, two summers and no winter, but that's not the way it is and you can't change it. Actually, we could change it if we moved Earth closer to the Sun or made our ozone layer thinner, but that is not what we would like to do, right?

You can complain about the winter, or you can prepare for the winter during the year. You can spend whole winter sitting hungry and cold complaining about your situation, or you can spend autumn preparing for the winter. You knew the winter will come. Everybody knows that, even small kids.

If you are a farmer and would like to have longer and warmer days instead of nights, you can build a greenhouse with artificial light. Change what you can and accept what you can't change.

Lesson learned: *Stop complaining and take full responsibility for your well-being. Study, analyze, think and make a long-term plan that you consider the best for you in your current situation. Split your long-term plan into short-term plans with your smaller achievable goals leading to your dreams. Follow the plan and check regularly if the situation has not changed and if you do not have to adapt your plan. Celebrate each small success to keep your motivation high.*

Get simpler

The winner in you asks 'How can I do it?' Don't

become too intelligent, because too-intelligent people always try to find a reason why it can't be done. Get more primitive and focus on how **it can** be done. If you know what you want, you can always find how to get it by studying. After you study it, prepare a plan and then simply follow the plan.

The loser in you finds excuses why it will not work. Winner will start with small steps and in the end, by being resilient; he will get what he wants. If you are too intelligent, it is harder for you to be successful as you will face many doubts, which prevent you from taking action. Simpler people don't have so many doubts and it is easier for them to reach their dreams. If I can change my rational and analytical approach to simple belief, I will do it. Simple things work the best.

Your habits

Your habits are the base for your character. Let's say, you have decided to exercise each morning. If your habit is to wake up and do exercise each morning, with each morning you become more disciplined and healthier. After a few months you will become a disciplined person even if you were not in the beginning. If you wake up and don't exercise that morning, with each morning you don't, you become a lazier person.

Yes, you can always find suitable excuse not to exercise. With controlling your habits you shape your character. Remember that self-made rich people consider who they are more important than what they have. They shape their character if needed. Step by step you can shape your character by copying habits of successful people and become successful character yourself. Once you become a successful character, your success will soon follow you. You will be destined for success.

Good thing about habits is that each time you perform your habitual action, it becomes easier and easier for you. It is like a flywheel – hard to start, but easier to keep in movement with each spin. When your action becomes a habit, it will be easy for you to perform that action without thinking and without losing much energy on that action.

Create a weekly schedule, where you will spend your time on studying and understanding, planning, working, exercising, relaxing and spending your time with people you love. Our bodies love repetitive schedule – for example going to bed at the same time each night and waking up at the same time each morning is good for your sleep and energy. Yes, even on weekends. Your body sets its internal clock and knows what to expect from you each day. The same goes for exercising – first few times it is difficult to do it, but after it becomes your habit, your body will welcome the exercise and you won't have to push yourself to do it.

If you want to be successful, you have to define what success is for you and ask yourself if you really want this. Everything gives you something and takes something from you. Also understand WHY you want this. Why is usually bound with your emotions and emotions give you motivation and energy. If you understand your WHY, you can always find a way HOW to do it.

When you have clear picture of what you want to achieve, write it down as a goal and use pictures to visualize it. Then make your habit to visualize what you want each morning. This way you will manipulate your brain for choosing the most important activities to reach that vision. With sinking into your day to day tasks it is easy to lose focus on your final goal. Make it your habit to remind yourself of what you want to achieve long-term.

Strong will, hard work

Which habits do you consider necessary to have to reach your goal? Choose habits that will help you to be more effective and productive and act as if you already had those habits. Good habits are your friends; bad habits are your enemies.

Self-discipline is the most important habit for success. It allows you to start and finish your plan. Best definition of self-discipline I could find: *'Self-discipline is the ability to make yourself do what you should do and when you should do it, whether you feel like doing it or not.'*

Get your work done quickly, don't waste your time. Focusing on the important stuff and leaving the other stuff behind helps you to work smart instead of working hard. An employed person who works hard can be rewarded or not. It depends on the company culture and his boss. In most big companies, the most recognized employee is not the one who works hardest, but the one who spends most time with his boss talking about what he did. What's important is to create the image in your boss's head of how valuable you are for him and for the company.

Many times people ask: "What is more important for success? Strong will or imagination?" In my experience it is imagination. Strong will is important but imagination is even more important than strong will. Day dreaming and imagination are essential. Look five or more years forward into the future and see things as they can be. When you seek your vision of future, you don't have to see the future just as it is. With your vision you can see it as it could be. Make your blurry vision absolutely clear and know what it will look like when you reach it. And of course write your vision down.

Many people talk about their great business idea but they don't take the action to start it. In my mind there are now two very close friends – one is my cousin and second is my neighbor. My cousin Martin and my second friend Marek are very smart, skillful and intelligent persons and they are very different. I love talking to them as I learn much from them every time. Actually they are prototypes of successful young men. One is married, lives in a house and works out. Other is single, lives in one of his flats and he likes to drink wine a lot. Both have ideas for successful businesses. They are very capable and I have no doubt, that if they would start those businesses, they will be successful. Unfortunately they haven't so far stepped out of the area of having the right ideas to area of doing them. If they would take action, they will be on the right path because they are smart and would take corrective actions if something went different than it was written in their plans.

Successful business people are not the ones who have the best ideas. It is those, who best realize those ideas. It helps if you are the first person to come with the idea, but there are lot of examples that even when you start last and you do your business better than the market leader, you will become the market leader. You don't have to be first to start, you have to be the best.

Importance of thinking and being smart is overrated

If you are like my cousin or Marek, you have two options to improve your financial situation – you have to become more primitive or you have to become more bold. In what I learned, IQ has very small influence on your success. It actually slows you down when you want to start. This means, lots of smart people have great businesses ideas, but they do nothing to implement them.

I found out, the smarter you are, the bolder you have to become to start. If you are too smart, you think too much and don't act. You have to understand, that good action following a good plan will be more successful than a great idea followed by no action. This is why we see a lot of 'primitive' people with lots of money and 'intelligent' people like academic teachers with less money. If you are 'too intelligent,' you spend much of your time thinking why your plan could not work and how to prevent it from not working. This is stopping you from taking action, as you are afraid to make a mistake.

Stop it. Stick to basics. If your plan works in basic principles, it is worth trying in action. Start your plan and if there should be some unpredicted problems (of course there will be some unpredicted problems, there always are), you will solve them on the go. They can't stop you. Keep moving. Break this obstacle by solving it, or find a way around. Don't stop once you start. Moving gives you energy.

It is great to have academic education, but to understand the basic principles, all you need is high school education. But only through experience you will find which theoretical principles work in day to day reality and which do not. Experience is not gained by reading books. For taking action, it is more important **if** it works and not **why** it works.

Academic education can help you in understanding why and how. It is important for understanding why things happen and also by visiting college you will build your social network of fellow students. This network is even more important in practical life than what you learned at school. If you are good observer and you study your subjects of interest, only reason why you should go to college is to get your social network and to find answers, which you did not find in those books or on the internet. There is not much knowledge in colleges, which is not already also online. The reason to go to college is to spend your time with people who are there.

Many teachers educate based on what they read in books and not what they experienced firsthand. They read lots of books and then they teach what they read without having firsthand experience. Academics tend to find 100% correct answers and to seek the ultimate truth. But in reality there are lots of truths. Every single person has his box of experience in his mind and he has his own set of truths. We all know that markets don't behave only in logical ways and they don't follow economic models all the time.

Simplified example for academic teacher versus professional teacher is that academic teacher will give you 100% correct answer which is 50 pages long and takes into consideration many variables. Professional teacher gives you a one sentence answer which is correct 90% of the time. Or he gives you a five-sentence answer which works 95% of the time if you are interested in details. Academic teacher gives you answer how things should be, professional teacher gives you answer how things really are.

For example I have been taught that high

market competition lowers the prices for the customer and increase quality of goods. This was considered solid fact on academic soil. But the reality is that prices of goods can also increase all the time due to inflation caused by our governments and banks and in order to survive the competition. Producers have to lower the quality of goods to keep production costs low with marketing costs increased to be able to stay on the market. It is the value of those goods that go down, but due to inflation the prices go up. It is not economically logical, but it happens.

An example of this is a story I heard from wholesale food producer. While he was in the process of negotiation, with a big international supermarket company purchaser in 2007 in Slovakia, the purchaser asked him for sausages, that cost 10 crowns (on average they cost 12-15 crown at that time). His producer told him that he can produce sausages at this price, but there will be almost no meat in them. But the supermarket purchaser was clear – 'I want sausages for 10 crowns.' The supermarket made nice promotional leaflets sent to each house saying how cheap their sausages were, and people purchased them. Other producers and supermarkets, to stay on the market, had to lower the quality of their own products. So the quality went down and due to inflation and high marketing costs the prices went up later back to 12 crowns when the special offer expired.

In a monopoly environment strange things can happen – with big amount of costs gone (the marketing costs), you can lower customer prices and increase quality of produced goods. This could happen. A more realistic situation in my opinion is that the top management of that monopoly company would drain those increased monopoly profits from the company into their own pockets. They would just reallocate the capital, we could say. They do it, for example, through other private companies, which sell their service to the big monopoly company or through mentioned "kickback" at advertising. It often happens that the service is never delivered and it is just signed as delivered on paper. Delivery of services is harder to control. Best are the IT systems as most people do not understand them.

What you can do to **become more primitive**?

- **Simplify everything.** Use *digital approach* – 0 – it works. 1 – it does not work. If something works, use it. If it doesn't work, change it or don't use it. It's not your job to understand how everything works. Leave 'why it works' to specialists or scientists. Your job is to take the profit and run.

- **Don't think too much.** If you have a plan, don't wait until it is perfect. A good plan in use is a hundred times better than a great plan which will never start its realization.

- **Trust your gut.** If you know yourself and understand your needs and wants, listen to your gut and act upon what you feel is the right thing to do.

What you can do to **become bolder?**

- Burn the go-back ship. You can for example tell your plan to a) somebody who will support you or to b) somebody who will make fun of you if you go back or fail. It must be somebody who is important for you so it is harder for you to tell him you failed. It is harder to give up now because you know, his/hers opinion about you can change if you give up. This will increase your commitment.

- Make sports, martial arts, activities where you will be afraid and where you will overcome your fear. With sports you support your winning attitude and experience the feeling of winning and losing. The same goes for martial arts even if you compete against yourself and not somebody else.

- Seek unpleasant situations and get used to them. It can be to initiate a small talk with beautiful stranger and asking him/her for a phone number. It can be taking unpleasant task in your community on your shoulders, which nobody else wants to do like cleaning sidewalks etc.

Time management, wasting time and focusing on priorities

Each morning look at your action plan and write down the goals you have to reach that day. Don't work just for sake of working. It is the results that matter. It is smart to prioritize your tasks and start your day with those which have the biggest impact on your results. Focus on results of the day and start with the task with the highest impact. You can do other lower level activities later if there is some time left. Do it even if you don't feel like starting the day with the most critical activity, because you are afraid that you need more time to prepare for the important task. Don't spend half the day 'starting yourself up' for the really important task. You can do it as your first activity and you will do it correctly even if you start your day with it. Never give yourself the luxury of first handling the small insignificant tasks. ALWAYS start with the most important task - the TASK OF THE DAY. Small tasks can grow during the day and you will not be able to start and finish what is really important.

When there are multiple tasks to handle and you don't know which is the most important, ask yourself following questions: Which of my tasks have the greatest impact on my key performance indicators? What is the reason I am on the payroll? Which activity, which only I am competent to do, has a critical influence on company's success?

Sometimes, mostly when you start new task, which you have never done before, you will be scared to start it, because you don't know how to do it. That's why you should put preparation on your to do list planed in advance. You can study, you can ask for an advice and then you do it. Don't be paralyzed by fear of failure. In real life you can't prepare for every situation, so don't spend time only preparing and preparing. Without doing the action, there will be no results. When your deadline is close and you have to do the new task, do it. Trying and doing something is better than postponing the task to infinity. Finish one task and then start the next one on your priority list. Even computers freeze when they do too much multitasking. Don't overload yourself with unfinished tasks.

Make a list your time consumers. You can list them like a budget – how much time does it take and what it gives you in return. You will soon find out that watching TV or killing your time on Facebook or internet porn takes a lot of time, but is giving you nothing back except maybe for frustration. Good news is that if you don't yet have sufficient discipline, you can use help like internet blocking software, unsubscribing from cable TV etc. Most of the time nothing important happens in the News, so you can stop watching it. Try it for a month. If something important happens, people around will tell you, don't worry. Limit your e-mail time to once a day. If it will be urgent, you will get a phone call.

Example of daily schedule

Wake up one hour earlier. If you have to leave your house for work/school at seven, wake up at six. This will give you great start for the day. Successful people work while others have fun. First thing in the morning you will work on yourself, and then you will work in your job or study at school. You are your most important asset. Visualize what you want today. You will get what you expect to get.

6:00 Wake up and first thing to do is to drink glass of water with freshly squeezed lemon. Do exercise with open window (When it is cold keep moving. When you stop moving, close the window so that you won't catch cold.). Take a shower changing cold and hot water. Practice breathing and visualize your successful day. Be grateful for what you already have. Have a breakfast.

6:30 Move to the office.

7:00 Prepare schedule of the day and start with the most important task. Don't waste your time reading e-mails or browsing internet. You can reply to your e-mails after the lunch. Focus on the most important task of the day first. Don't allow other people or other tasks to distract you from your daily most important task until it is done.

You should have light snack containing of fresh salad or other greens during short break.

11:00 Have a break for a slow and healthy lunch and spend as much time on fresh air and the sun as you can. Don't eat too much or it will make you sleepy. Avoid sweets, they are not good for a fighter. Sweets make your metabolism unbalanced.

12:00 Work, work, work. Check your e-mails and reply to them, but limit the time spent on e-mails it under 20 minutes. When you feel hungry, have light and healthy snack again.

16:00 Have a short break and think about your day – have you been productive? Have you come closer to your goals? Make necessary corrections and continue working.

16:30-17:30 Go to your training. Choose one sport and become the best at it. If you don't have training at that day of the week, you can work on yourself. Learn a foreign language, work or train your head with other tools.

19:00-20:00 Go home to your family or visit your friends. Shop for groceries and keep your room clean and tidy. Don't watch TV. Spend your time talking to people, not playing with computer or your phone. Smile a lot, life is beautiful. Relax and do whatever you want to do. Don't watch or read news – you will become influenced by the negative reports and you will find nothing important there. If something important happens in the world, people around will tell you.

22:00 Summarize your beautiful and productive day, be thankful for the possibility to have it and go to bed.

On weekends keep the wake up time and most of all go to bed time the same as during the work week. Have one day in a week clean of your duties if possible. Go to the nature, enjoy the sun and be thankful for your life and your health. Then do whatever you feel like doing.

Money, debt and risks

Having money is better than not having money. That is a fact. If you have more than you need, you can always give it to someone. But if you don't have enough money, it is much harder to find someone who will give it to you without receiving something from you in exchange. Only issue with having more money than you need is that you can start spending them on things you don't need. If you stay disciplined, there is no problem with too much money.

Don't lose money. Every time you reach next financial level you should lock it in an asset. You can lock that level with cash and asset management and very good insurance. Don't waste money showing off how rich you are unless you want to attract people who will be with you because of your money.

You can be happy and still have lot of money. Money can't buy you happiness, but it can help you live life that you desire and thus become happy. Money can't buy you a health, but it can buy you best possible healthcare. Money can't buy you love, but not having enough money for normal living standards can cost you your loved one. Most common reason of divorce is fights because of lack of money or because different opinions about their usage. You have to know how much your desired life standard cost you and then make sure, you will have enough money from your assets to pay for it.

Ask yourself "What kind of person do I have to become to have that amount of money?" If you don't know, look at your role models, what kind of person are they. Study them and become one of them.

Debt. One definition of money is that *Money is debt*. This is true. With our monetary and banking system, money is created from thin air against somebody's decision to be in debt to the bank. With fractional reserves, those debts can't be paid back all at once. Much of that money is virtual and because of interest rates, the debt will be always higher than the money in the circulation. This information could lead to an idea, that money is scarce as there is not enough money.

But the truth is a completely different story. Money is abundant and as long as you persuade banks that you will be able to pay back the money with interest, they will create new money for you. With inflation and the added value you create, you are able to pay back your debt with interest and still make a profit. Because an average person can't control the inflation, you have to focus on creating added value. It can be the value of your product or service, the value of your capital gain, or the value of the intellectual property you created.

Just like banks are legally allowed to create money out of thin air, you are legally allowed to create money from your realized ideas which you sell to the market. Borrow money only to purchase assets and only after your calculations show it will still be profitable even if not everything goes according to your plans. Don't buy anything on credit unless it is assets. If you don't have enough money without borrowing, admit you can't afford it **yet**. Ask yourself "How can I afford it?" If you really want it, first purchase assets that will pay for that item.

Risks. When you borrow some money, there is always risk that you will not be able to pay it back with interest or to pay it back at all. Some people plan in advance to use loopholes in the law and before they borrow money, they plan not to pay it back. That is the reason why you have to ask to be paid an interest when you lend money to someone else – always ask for interest. When you lend money without interest, you are losing control and interest which you could get when put to bank account. Because money value is bound with time, it can happen easily, that money you don't need today, will be needed to cover your costs in the future before the payback time. Because you lent it to someone, you will not be able to pay your costs and you can get into trouble.

Lend money only if you are 99% sure, you will not need it and always ask for interest rate and the collateral. It happened to me multiple times that loan I made was due, but the person did not return my money. Always put penalties for late payment into your contract. Think about time in your contracts – if you will not be paid your money and interest back, how much time and energy will it cost you to get your money back, with court and distrainment? Will the profit be worth the trouble?

Is the interest rate you ask in your contract covering those possibilities? If you win in court and pay all the costs, will the person have enough assets or money to pay you back? Courts can take a few years. During that time your debtor can become a person with no money and assets, so even if you have a court decision in your hands, it does not mean you will get your money back.

Yes, even if you know the person you lend money to is your friend, he may not pay you back. It happened to me multiple times and I almost lost friend. He paid it back, but I will never lend him money again.

Accounting, numbers and analyzing assets

First of all you need to know where you are with your money, assets and liabilities. What kind of debts you have and how it affects your cash flow. Determine your net worth, your monthly average cash flow, split your monthly spending into groups, and evaluate your assets and liabilities. After seeing your numbers you should have a clear picture how healthy your finances are. Most important indicator of your financial health is not how much you earn or how much you spend, but how much you keep for investing. This means to sum all your monthly incomes and subtract all your monthly spending.

Monthly spending can be split into groups like housing costs, nutrition cost, transport/car costs, taxes costs, insurance costs, presents, education costs, entertainment costs, hobby costs, sport costs, healthcare costs and investment costs. Know where you spend money and how much you spend there. This will help you stop money leaking away on things you don't really need. Measure at least for a month every single spent dollar and mark it down to appropriate group in your sheet. This process helped me to realize that I spend lot of cash on presents. I love giving presents to people who are important to me. But spending 14% of all my spending including housing, transport and food just on presents was too much. I did not realize that before I started to write down every spent cent. You will be maybe also surprised where your money goes.

Month	Monthly income	Monthly spending	Monthly cash flow
January			
February			
March			
April			
May			
June			
July			
August			
September			
October			
November			
December			
Average value			
Sum			

After one month of your personal accounting you will know if your spending is alright or if you need to close some money leaks - or spend more on something like education or sport. My recommendation is to do it for a year as during the Christmas period your gift spends increases and during summer usually holiday spending increases. If you are not satisfied with what you see, make a monthly spending budget and put a monthly limit to each spending group. Regularly summarize how much you spent on which group and how close are you to your monthly spending limit.

If you managed to hold your spending budget within the limits, reward yourself. It can be pat on your back or you can buy yourself something you really wanted – of course, within your budget limits.

Put aside at least 10% of all your income to investment account. Do it as a first money operation after you receive money. Consider that money not yours. Think of it as money belonging to other people, who have put their cash into your investment fund: you have to multiply it, or at least not lose it. Do not allow yourself to use that money on anything else but buying assets. If you are saving money for big asset and it takes time to save enough, protect your money against inflation. Most savings accounts in banks have lower interest rates than the inflation. This means that by saving money, you can be losing money. If possible, put your money into assets which protects the value of your money. The usual advice is to buy real estate, gold and silver. But even real estate, gold and silver can lose financial value because of speculation.

Having money on your bank account is still

considered to be the safest way to store it. Generally, precious metals are considered safe when compared to currency money. New currencies like Bitcoin are still considered risky investment. There are fluctuations on the market, expect that price can go down after you buy.

Before you purchase gold or silver, study purchasing and selling gold and silver, make a plan which also has an exit strategy. Always have in mind that you should purchase when something is cheap and sell it when it is expensive. Stick to your plan and don't follow the crowd. Take your time to make decisions about purchasing and selling. Don't buy or sell based on your current emotion but on numbers. If you have bad feeling of the investment, don't invest. If someone is pushing you to investment and you don't have good feeling about this person or investment, don't invest. If the investment sounds too good to be true, it probably is. You can easily lose money if you don't know how to protect your investment. Read the small print in contracts and learn to play 'What if?'

- What if the person won't keep the conditions of the contract?
- What if the person disappears? How will I get my money back?

General rule is to spend as much time on studying and analyzing investment, as you spent on earning money for that investment. Most important question to ask is: **How will you get your money with interest back from the investment?**

Delay all big spending until you have enough time to think about them. Do you really need that new couch, car, gun or gold coins? Do I need a new item? You can often find an used item of higher quality for a lower price.

Distinguish facts from opinions and verify 'facts' that other people give you. People giving you 'facts' can be wrong or they can even consciously lie to you. Even people of high social rank can lie – look at politicians. They will tell us everything is alright, don't panic and then they move their money out of the country like they did in Cyprus, because they know a few days later they are going to rob people of their money in bank accounts. If politicians try to calm down the masses, there is probably some scam behind it.

Until you can't verify the fact, it is just an opinion. Act based on facts if possible. Postpone your decision if your partner puts pressure on you. There will be other opportunities to invest, don't worry.

Before you enter the investment, do the following steps:

1. Write down rules of your exit strategy. These are rules that protect you from losing money spent on investment. Implement those rules into your deal.

2. Have a plan how to protect your asset. It can be insurance, control, trade mark etc.

3. Have a plan how you will manage and control your asset. For example by having sent financial statements to you every month and putting rules into deal, which will guarantee you control to make necessary changes if the asset is not giving you what you agreed on.

4. Have rules implemented in your deal telling how and when the asset you just purchased will give you your money with interest back. Implement the sanctions for late payments.

Mentors and role models

Seek mentors and role models. You do not have to meet them in person to use their ideas. Good books, like <u>Kyiosaki's Rich Dad, Poor Dad</u> can help you when you are not sure what to do. <u>Jim Collins</u> is my favorite book mentor. I have never met him, but I read their books sometimes and when in doubt, I ask myself, what would Jim do if he were in my situation. Parents are your role models whether you like it or not. Your friends can be your role models. People around you can motivate you for better actions or for worse actions.

Who you spend your time with determines your future. Consciously make the effort to learn from successful leaders and investors if you want to be rich. Learn from your rich or successful friends and tell them how you admire what they did. There is nothing bad about it.

Do you know who can stop you from being successful except you? It is surprising, but it is the people who love you and care about you. They don't want you to make mistakes. They don't want to see you feeling bad, so they overprotect you from trying risky activities. They will try to persuade you why you should not do it. They have good intentions; however, their good intentions can stop you and that's why you should keep your ambitious plans for yourself. This is very important while you are in a phase where you are still not decided if you will realize of your dream or not.

Questions to ask yourself:

Question	Answer
What is my inner genius?	
Whom should I meet with to grow my character?	
What environment should I be in to develop my genius?	

The rich you

It is not what you have, but who you become that decides if you will be rich or not. Ask yourself if you are willing to change your habits, learn and work hard on yourself to become rich. Each activity is usually hard in the beginning. In the end it will be easy for you, but beginnings are usually difficult. If you dedicate yourself to become rich person, you will be. Everyone who desired it and never quit, made it. It is a sure path.

Characteristics of successful people are ambitious determination, discipline and self-esteem.

If you have those characteristics, there is nothing you can't achieve. Work hard on improving and polishing those characteristics in you and you will become person with no limits.

First of all you have to become the most effective you can be. You don't want to become rich after 70 years of work, but a lot sooner. The more effective your actions, the more you will accomplish in a shorter time. Ask yourself: "In what area do I have to **become great** to achieve wealth?" Read biographies of wealthy people and look for their personal characteristics. What are they like? How do they think? Be ambitious-realistic and understand that usually they show only their nicer part in the books. There is high probability they have bad habits too and have done 'not so good' things. I have bad habits too and I have done bad things in the past. Everybody makes errors in judgment. Wealthy people are not so much different from you or me. They have to sleep, eat and visit the bathroom just like we do. They are ordinary humans doing ordinary things extraordinary well.

If you want to become a self-made millionaire, you have to be ambitious. In the beginning, you will have to work while others relax. That will give you an advantage over the average person. You will have to work a lot, but it does not mean you will have to work hard. If you love what you do, it will not be that hard. With time you will become used to working a lot and it will be normal for you. You will not understand how other people can waste their time without having bad feelings. There are two types of successful people – hard workers and passionate ones. **Hard workers** who wanted to become wealthy, make a plan and stick to it with discipline. They work even if they are tired or if they hate the work that needs to be done. As soon they understand that it needs to be done, they stop thinking whether they like to do it or not, they just do it. **Passionate ones** work also a lot, but to them work which needs to be done is also passion and fun.

The highest percentage of successful self-made rich people, have done it being a good businessman or an investor. Dedicate some of your time to education and practice in finances and investing. Start small with investing or business if you are not willing to take big risks, losses and wins and you haven't done this successfully few times before. Recommended small businesses to start with are network marketing businesses or franchise businesses as they give you a system on which to operate your business.

With good network marketing education program you will learn and experience how to sell, how to handle rejection, how to stop worrying what others will think of you and you will learn how to lead and manage people.

There are many network marketing companies out there and they are not equal. Some are making rich only the people on the top. Some will help you to become rich yourself. When choosing your network marketing company, look for one which has a successful history. Find and ask people who left that company for what reason they left it. Then find out if you are comfortable with their reward system and if people there are the ones you want to work with. Only after those criteria are met, look at the product. It is the system you want to understand and learn. They can have a great product, but if the system and the people there are not right for you, you will struggle. If you have more money to start with, you can purchase a franchise license. The franchisor will show you how to do it right by giving you his system.

Studying is not enough!

You have to get painful experience to grow.

To get usable knowledge you have to both read and practice. Reading is only the first part of the learning process. To learn the important things you will have to do them. It will probably hurt in the learning process, because you make mistakes. Mistakes that hurt are natural learning tools in human life. Do not expect that you will make no mistakes, everybody does.

This is why you should start small and then grow your business or investments. You don't want to get hurt beyond repair. If you do not have the needed knowledge and experience with that type of asset, start small. You have to learn how to crawl before you learn how to run. By starting small, I mean invest only as much as you can afford to lose without breaking your self-esteem if the investment blows up. Be prepared. It will blow up and you will have to rebuild it again without the mistake which blew it up. This can happen a few times until your asset will be profitable sustainably. Start small, test that what you are doing is profitable, and only then grow it. This small business is like a prototype for you and when it works on a small scale, you can grow it bigger and conquer the world.

For example, I made that mistake when we purchased product from a new Chinese supplier. I was in a hurry to get that product to Europe and I did not send the inspection to check the production. We had already paid 30% deposit and I did not expect the malfunction rate to be above 10%. It looked smarter to risk losing 10% with malfunctions then a 30% deposit.

However, after a few months the malfunction rate came up to 36%! What a mistake! That pressure from lost money pushed me and my colleagues to think. He came up with an idea using special silicone to make them more durable. I hired friends to repair each product in a warehouse. Every product that left our warehouse was tested and we reduced malfunctions to 5%, which was caused mostly by inappropriate handling by the customer.

Don't blame yourself too long when you make a mistake. Make disappointment your strength. All mistakes will make you feel bad, but mistakes you learn from make you smarter. Mistakes where you didn't learn anything about how to prevent the same mistake from happening again will make you only feel bad. The more mistakes you make, the more experience you will get. The more experience you have, the more you can trust your gut when making decisions.

If your mother told you not to touch that hot pot, because you can burn yourself, has it been imprinted on your mind not to touch hot pot? Probably yes, but the lesson is never so alive as if you learn it from experiencing it first hand and touching the hot pot. You feel the pain and it programs your body to watch out for hot pots from now on. When you go near the hot pot with your hand, your sub-conscious mind keeps your hand from touching the hot pot again. What had the deeper influence on your learning process? When someone told you not to do something, or when you did it and got hurt?

We live in era of the information age. It is the action based on the knowledge and information that makes you rich faster. But having information is not enough. You have to have knowledge about how to profit from that information and you have to act based on that information and knowledge.

Learn to handle your failures and successes

Solving problems makes you stronger. As we grow older, we solve bigger and bigger problems and that's why we see problems from our past as small or insignificant and we solve them easily. Each bad thing that happens to you teaches you a lesson - if you are ready to watch, analyze it and learn.

There is an old saying, *"If someone is throwing wooden logs under your feet to make it harder for you, take the logs and make fire of them."* Sometimes you can make your biggest failure into your biggest success if you change your point of view.

Most self-made millionaires started from zero and made that zero into millions. Many of them lost the millions and went back to zero again. Really successful people took the zero, analyzed it, and turned it into next million. As they learned from their loss, they got stronger and smarter with their second million.

When you are poor, it is not because what happened to you, but what you did about what happened to you. I saw on YouTube one guy who has no legs and arms. His name is Nick Vujicic. He has no hands and legs, but he jumps around and even dives in the pool. He did not give up as most people would and he became famous. This guy is amazing. He makes fun of his handicap. The important lesson is that people can do miracles, if they dedicate their life to do them.

It is not what happens to you that decide your destiny. It is "***What you do with what happens to***

you is what decides your destiny." There is another old and truthful saying "***Everything bad that happens to you is good for something.***" Your life is giving you lessons. The harder the lessons, the stronger you become. Look at children of many rich people – if they don't have to try hard, because their path was cleared of any obstacles by their parents, they become weak. They haven't got opportunities to learn from hard times or from solving big financial problems.

Necessity does not push their inner genius to evolve. They simply don't have to try that hard. From lack of work and from abundance of resources they were given, they sometimes even don't know what to do with their free time. Some even start to use narcotics as they do not see any reason to live and they seek some stimulation. If you are responsible and have some duties, you won't allow yourself to take narcotics, because then you could not fulfill those duties. With those duties you have reason to live and you don't have time for such things. Parents are excellent example – they have to take care of their kids, they have a reason to live and if they are mentally and physically healthy, they will never give up. They can't because they are responsible for someone. It is responsibility that makes us stronger.

Another great example is of an old woman who got cancer. She was about to die in a few months. Her son told her, "Hey mom, you can't die. You have to take care of your grandson's wedding in few years." And she recovered. The problem with cancer disappeared and she arranged her grandson's wedding. A few months after the wedding, she died. She fulfilled her life purpose and the cancer came back. Everybody should find his reason to live. Find your reasons by understanding yourself. Knowing and understanding yourself is one of your most important tasks in your life. Character building experiences will help you with it. Go and search for them. Find out what you are made of - test your limits. If you never try them, you will never find out what you are capable of.

There is nothing that can stop you from achieving what you dream of, except for yourself and death. If you are ready to die, there is only you yourself who can give you limits. Nobody else can. We all are going to die once. It is normal, but even people who want to go to heaven don't want to die. This is also normal, because of our self-preservation instincts. Nobody physically and mentally healthy wants to die.

If person learns how to conquer his fears (e.g. fear of death) and realize there are no limits except those which he makes himself, he is free to do what he wants.

You will make mistakes and that's alright

Remember that everybody who is doing something new makes mistakes. The road to glory is littered with problems - and problems solving. When you do something new (and today's business happens so fast, that you'll almost always be doing something new), you will make mistakes. Get used to it. What's important is to learn from your mistakes, and to take corrective action immediately. For example having a bad business partner will teach you more than having a good partner. I do NOT advise you to find a bad partner. But if it happens to you, take it as a costly training and as a given opportunity to learn. You will learn how to recognize who is the bad partners for you and you can avoid them next time. Bad business partner for you does not mean he is a bad person. It just means that you are not compatible to work together. He or she can be a very good partner for someone else.

It is almost like playing a computer role playing game – you train your virtual character, increase its abilities and when your virtual character gets killed, you just reload the game. By the end of the game, you have an impressive virtual character and you are probably proud of it. But when you turn off the computer, your strong, experienced and well-equipped 'virtual you' is no more. If you spent that time to increase *your* experience, stamina or strength, instead of that of your virtual character, would that not have a better influence on your life? If two of ten kids spent their evening running and jumping compared to the eight kids running their virtual character on a computer, who will be the best? If you are the one of those two who spend their evenings outside, you can be the best runner from the whole group. And you will get the priceless experience of overcoming obstacles.

For adults there is the example of watching sports on TV, as against doing sports for real. 80% of people never take the harder way. You can get to the top 20% just by deciding to take the hard way. Don't waste your time becoming the best in your virtual world, become the best in the real world, because that is what counts in the end. If you want to be happy, dedicate your life to something and become the best at it.

When something bad happens to you, look closer, it can be a hidden blessing

Anger can be useful if directed the right way and the bad things that happen to you can be used as character building experiences. Use them for your profit. "Nobody steals money from me without feeling my revenge" is what I promised myself at that time when somebody cheated me of my money. "I will make my money back multiple times and you will regret it."

My partner and I started the new company and we put all of our money together and purchased goods from China and began to sell them. Each day we learned something new and improved our business. Everything was well for a few months.

Because I had only one quarter share of company (I lacked investment capital at that time to make it 50/50 business), soon my partner started to break the agreement we had about controlling the money, and our rows began. After a year or so I resigned as I knew I could not gain control over cash flow and my partner was cheating me. I asked him to either sell me his part of company or to buy mine. It was not a pleasant process to negotiate the price and decide who was to purchase whose share. I wanted to have no more contact with him, so I sold mine. We signed the deal and he was supposed to pay me within a month. I knew he was used to paying later than agreed, so there was interest on late payment in the contract. I waited for a month and I was deleted from company register as a partial owner, but the money did not come.

I heard many excuses but I knew my partner was a liar, so I did not accept them. He was a very good liar, I have to admit. Once he said to me: "I am a businessman. I will tell you what you need to hear to do what I want." It is truth that some businessmen do that, but they are not the honest businessmen. I have to admit that my ex-partner is not honest, but he still is a successful businessman. I have read many books on business development and they all say - you have to be honest to be successful. It is not truth. You really don't have to be honest to be successful. You may be an honest businessman, but it will be harder for you. I will share a story where I understood how important is who you work with.

We were returning from a meeting once and my ex-partner was driving the car and wanted to switch to another lane, but there was a truck which would not let him. He got angry and used the emergency lane to get in front of the truck and he told me he was going to stop it. Stopping a fully loaded truck is not easy and I thought he was joking so I said "Go ahead if you wish". I could not believe he was going to do it for real. He blocked the truck, but the truck driver did not see us. Since his cab and his seat were much higher than our car and we were out of his sight, he hit our car.

My partner grew red as he realized that he is in the driving lane he should not be in and that our car is pretty badly damaged. We all knew that it was my partner's fault and that our company would pay the damages. He could have had problems with the police. I told him to relax as nobody got hurt and only cars are damaged, it can be repaired. He looked desperate. After catching his breath, my partner started to persuade the truck driver not to call the police. We were blocking a very important road and were causing a traffic jam. My partner and the truck driver reached agreement within ten minutes and we left.

The next day I heard how my colleague was describing the accident to someone else. Suddenly it was not the Slovak truck driver, it was a Polish truck driver and it was the entire truck driver's fault and my partner was the poor victim. He was so persuasive, that if I had not been in that car and I had not seen what really happened, I would have believed him for sure. At first I thought he was speaking about a completely different car accident, but I knew he was lying. When something like this happens, the liar changes the picture of what happened in his mind so that he looks good to himself and puts all the blame on someone else. Then he repeats his altered story in his mind until he starts to believe it. And then he tells the altered story to others with the belief that it really happened like he is telling. It is hard to find out he is lying, because he really believes what he is saying.

I knew from that time on I didn't want to do business with him anymore. Money is not worth of being constantly lied to. If he can lie so well to others, he is lying that good to me as well.

Because the money for my share of the company was still not paid to my account, I searched for some enforcement companies to get the money for me. As they were using only legal actions and my ex-partner knew how the legal system works, I was not paid for quite a long time. Later, with help of my uncle, he paid me approximately one third and few months later the second third of all the money. Law was on my side, but law enforcement was not working. I had to pay 6% of that money he owned me as the court fee just to start the court acting. It is now for more than one year and based on my lawyer's experience I will get a court decision with all the tricks of multiple revalidations from the side of my ex partner within two years.

After two years I will have to pay 10% to the executor who will collect the debt if my ex-partner does possess any assets. He has already hidden our previous company behind another company, so this could be quite a problem. If he officially does not own anything for ten years, my claim will be called due and he will get away with it. As I am not willing to take any illegal actions since the money is not worth of it, he will get off without paying. But still there is hope. I will see in few years how it ends.

After I got some money back, I changed the core business of my other company to an online shop. To speed up selling I have been using ClickEshop instead of some free CMS. It helped me to forget the IT tasks and focus solely on online marketing. Mr. Vajda and his team were quick to develop and implement my requests. I can only recommend ClickEshop team.

I sold the company a few weeks ago after two years of operations because I had grown tired of it. I also wanted to have six to twelve months holiday to recharge my batteries. The path to success is usually not straight and I started this company intending to consult on internet sales. However my own online shop looked more profitable with a higher return on investment, so I changed its core business. Having an online shop was not what I wanted, but revenge and my experience as an internet sales person allowed me to run it for two years. **You don't have to finish everything you start** – this is another valuable lesson I learned. If the path you started will not bring you to your desired location, don't continue that path.

Forex disaster

As my company was profitable and I had excessive cash flow, I searched for investment vehicles to get passive income. I was interested in

Foreign Exchange. I tested my results on demo accounts, but usually I lost my demo money in the long term. One man I knew from volleyball introduced me to another man during while playing snooker. I found out that he works for a forex trading company. He offered me a seminar on Forex. This man's name is Jozef. I saw how Jozef was doing his trading and after his seminar for Forex beginners, I decided that I could trust him as we had a common friend. After all, he told me he had been doing it for 12 years and they even had special Russian software which made a profit every year of more than 100%.

As the contract looked good and he was paid only by the profit he made, I decided to invest there. The deal was that I would give capital to be traded by this software and we would split profits 50/50. I said that was great because now I was sure Jozef would have great motivation to run my forex account well to get his profits, too. I had control over the account so I could watch it and withdraw the money any time I wanted. My thoughts were – I have a motivated and experienced partner, I have control over the investment, nothing can go wrong. But I did not have experience in dealing with people like Jozef. This investment was doomed to fail.

For the first month everything went well and I made nice profit of 10%. But the second month I lost 30% of the account value. As I had my exit strategy ready, I had to act when I lost 25% on that account next month. I took the money out. Jozef called me and he was furious. He persuaded me that this was normal and he never ever lost money. I made a mistake and trusted his word, so I put the remaining money back in that account. Within a month everything was gone.

Lesson learned: *Always and I mean always follow your exit plan. Don't trust people who tell you that you can trust them.*

The more they talk about how you can trust them, the less you should. Money I could have lived on comfortably for a year was gone. I was ruined. And I needed that money for my own company growth.

Well, it happens. Life goes on and you have to keep fighting. Every single businessman I know has experienced losses. There will be many disasters on the way to success and you have to overcome them. The bigger the problems you solve, the bigger person you will become. The first disaster always looks the worst of all. With time and experience you will learn how to handle them. Usually the biggest problems give you the most experience and courage to continue.

There are things you can't be taught by reading a book. You have to experience it in your own skin, be crushed and reshaped by that experience and then you will find a solution to that problem. For example, when we had many problems with products that got jammed, it has cost us a lot of money for a few months. It took me some time to figure out why the product jammed so often. When I found out, I stopped exchanging the goods when customer sent it back claiming he used it only once. Most of them lied because it could be seen it was used quite a lot. Usually after writing the customers a letter stating that they have not used it in compliance with manual and it is because of this that their product stopped working, they told the truth. It was hard to believe, but even customers can lie to you. The most common lie is that the product broke itself after one usage. I know it first hand, because I saw even my relative to do it when he claimed a refund.

Lesson learned: *Don't believe everything you are told or what you read.*

People do lie and even people with authority do lie if it is beneficial for them. I recommend you to read the book by John Virapen, – *"Side Effects: Death"*. You will understand that even your doctor can lie to you. And everybody, I hope, knows that politicians lie to us all the time. The same goes for other authorities like scientists, etc.

It was scientifically proven that people believe everything, which starts its sentence with term "It was scientifically proven". I was a scientist for few years during my PhD. study. Scientists are paid by grants and they know they need to direct their research results in a way which will allow them to receive another grant.

Always think about what you are being told and look for motives behind their words. Be a student but don't be a follower. Make your own conclusions. Compare what you are being told with other sources of information.

You have to stay calm during the catastrophe

When my company was in a law suit with our competition for trademark reasons, I received a letter from the competing company. As I read the charge, I nearly could not fall asleep that night. When I spoke with another businessmen a few months later, I learned that the usual thing you do when you receive your first serious looking law suit, is that you crap your pants. And the next day you contact your lawyer. The next day always looks brighter and you start to think. Trademark lawyers always put together suits that are many pages long just to show their customer how much work they have done. And they claim things they have no right to claim just to scare you. All you have to do is to breathe calmly and find a lawyer to look at the suit. If he is good, he will find holes in their suit, or at least he will tell you how to minimize the cost of that lawsuit. I have to admit we lost the case. I was happy that I was protected by my limited company and I could not go personally bankrupt. The worst that could happen was that I would lose all the money I had loaned to my company. I still would be healthy and could start again with more experience and knowledge. When you start a business, always and I mean always protect yourself through some sort of limited company.

High performance and relax

We had a saying in the AIESEC "Work hard, party hard." It means you have to balance hard work with relaxation. The smartest activity I have been able to figure out so far, is to do sports. You have only one body and the human body was created for movement and physical work. If you don't give your body enough physical work, it will not work very well and soon also your mental strength will become weaker, copying your physical strength. If possible, always have straight back not only in fights but all day long – it helps your belly breathing and it is good for your spine. There are exceptions, of course, and people who have such incredible metabolisms that they can work and work without having to care about their bodies. However for most people, this is not the case. If you spend 12 hours sitting behind the computer, you have to balance it with sports, or at least with walking.

It can be fun activities like building a snowman in the winter with your friends. If you are closed indoors during your work hours, balance it with activities outdoors after your work is done.

Continuous high performance is based on harmony between work and free time. Optimal work is the one which would you like to do even in your free time for free. You will not get tired easily in work which is your hobby at the same time.

If you feel tired working for a longer period of time, rest before you burn out. If you are asking yourself, "Why am I doing this?" stop and take your time to think it through. When you are just doing basic operations, you will not see the whole picture – what your dreams are and what makes you happy.

To prevent burning out learn to interest yourself with what you do. Look at your work as active holiday, an exercise to improve your skills and character, or as an adventure. If you don't like your work or you hate it, the best you can do is to find another job. Make a list of your free time activities. What do you like doing?

An example of what I like doing is teaching kick box to my friends, relaxing by giving massages or dancing, spending time with family, friends or even walking the dogs from a nearby animal shelter. I feel almost as lucky during those activities as I feel seeing I have created something of value. Relationships, satisfying work and sports are the basis for my happiness.

Three years ago I made a list of what I want to accomplish. There are items like being financially secure, comfortable and rich; being able to survive almost any situation, to have a good wife and children, and to finish a fantasy book I started when I was seventeen and postponed the writing of until I retire. Then I can die with knowing I have done everything I wanted in my life and thus by being prepared for death, I can be truly free.

I have made my finances secure and I can live comfortably whatever happens. I know who I am, who I am not, what I want to do and what I don't want to do, and this knowledge gives me power. I know that even if I go broke, I can start again and reach whatever goal I set my mind to. I have found out that owning things can give you a good feeling. I also have found out those things you are not able to let go possess you instead of you possessing them. Having more things than you want can make you less happy. I was less happy because I had skiing equipment sitting idle in my room. I spent money for something that I didn't need as I ski only once in two years. Instead of having a good feeling that I own them, I had a bad feeling that I wasted my money and that I wasted space in my room for something I didn't need.

How to spend your money

Good news is that you can buy everything you desire. You just can't buy liabilities before you buy assets. Postpone your spending and buy liabilities with money generated from your assets. Use your desire to accumulate assets first and buy what you desire as the reward for your discipline later. You can even use credit to purchase your desired item, but all monthly costs must be paid by your asset generated monthly positive cash-flow. If you desire a new cell phone that will cost you 50 dollars a month for two years, first acquire an asset which is generating more than 50 dollars a month in positive cash-flow for you or start a company which will buy it for you. Or save on your other spending items like food, entertainment, and use the 50 dollars you have saved to purchase your cell phone. What is important is that you keep as much money by the end of month as you planned to keep.

Some people say money is not important. It is simply not truth. We need to use money. It is a great exchange tool for what we need and want. Planning with money is easy, because you can count it. You can look at your bank account and know exactly how much do you have.

How to buy assets? Profit is made when you buy. The simple rule is that you have to buy at low price and sell at high price. First find out at which price you can sell and then go and find a good deal purchasing it cheaper. It is possible to buy at a low, usually wholesale price, use the product, and then sell it with profit. You will not find good deals for everything you purchase, but at least for expensive products look for a good deal. You have to consider also your time spent finding good deals. It is not wise to spend 2 hours and then save 50 cents when you could spend those 2 hours to earn 40 dollars. **Time is money**.

Investing takes time and experience to master it. First you have to crawl to learn how to run. I do not recommend doing big deal investments if you lack experience in this type of investment. If you spent five years doing those deals working for someone else, you have good experience by now. However, usually employees do only partial tasks, so it is wise to learn the whole process, if that is your case.

Develop the habit of investigating before you invest in anything. The rule is ***Spend as much time investigating the investment as you spent earning the money that you are thinking of investing***.

My recommendation is to do smaller deals when starting with investing. It will not hurt you so much when you lose the investment. Remember that you are still in the learning process, so you may make mistakes, which will cost you your money.

Rich people invest in their financial education or hire people who have the financial education and can be trusted. This is the difficult part – who can be trusted? You will find out by studying human nature and psychology and applying it in real life. In case studies it is very simple – a person is simply described and you can be very sure how they will act in a case study. Real life is more difficult and you need time to know the person. Even references from people you know can be faked and the referee can (and probably will) have different measures to evaluate his performance.

Investing tips:

- Suggested percentage of your income to invest is to put 10% of your income into assets. Increase the percentage if you can. I use 50 % right now.

- Pay yourself first. Always. Don't take out more money from the company if it needs them to grow, but pay yourself first, not your suppliers.

- Stay disciplined with your money – have a spending plan and delay gratification.

To transfer wealth from other people to yourself, you will have to use deals and money. Accumulating wealth by bartering is not usual these days. You have to understand what your feelings towards the money are. Think thoroughly about your opinion about money. What kind of people have a lot of money? Can you get what you want without the money or you have to use money to reach your goals? How much money do you need and how much do you want? What were you told and taught about the money?

What was your parents' approach to money in your childhood? Is money evil or is it good? You have to understand your money beliefs.

Money is neither good nor bad. It is just a tool like the fire or the knife. Money can help you and other people or it harm you or other people. It depends only on you how you will use it. Skill in earning and spending money is one of basic survival skills in an urban environment.

What do I know about money and how do I feel about money?

There are only a few people on our planet who live without money as our civilization is based on the exchange of goods and services through money. When dealing with money you have to know:

- how to "create" more money
- how to protect your money
- how to invest your money

Saving money and using money of others

I do not know anybody who got rich just by

saving money. In today's world money loses value by inflation and that's why it is not smart to save anymore. As we saw in the Cyprus case, government can take even 60% of what you have in your account whenever they decide to pass a law allowing them to do it. Savers are losing value stored in money every day, because central banks are printing more and more money which means you can buy less and less with nominal value of money. In the past, money had value, as the central banks promise was to exchange money for gold or silver. This principle is not true anymore. If you bring money to the bank, you will get nothing. For saving money you will get percentage of it, but this percentage is taxed and what you get is usually less than what you lose by inflation.

But even if money is losing value in today's banking system, we still need it to exchange goods and services. Just remember – storing wealth in money is an idea that will not make you rich unless your interest rate is higher than the inflation and you already are rich. If you have some extra money you can invest, purchase assets to create more money faster. First learn how to purchase, because there are lots of people who will scalp you and give you bad deals just to get a quick buck out of you. If you are, e.g. purchasing silver or jewels, find the wholesale dealer, as the margin of retail dealer can be as much as 600%.

Use your talents, money, resources and time to create assets. You can use talent, money, resources and time of other people. Remember that in today's world where money is not backed by real values, it is just a currency and if inflation is high, using the bank's money can be more profitable for you. You have to make all the calculations and see what is optimal for you.

Cash flow control

You have to make your cash flow positive. Once you have positive cash flow, exchange excessive cash for assets, which will bring you even more cash. Simpler said than done, right? Here is an example of a cash flow plan – for simplicity we will abstract from taxes and we will consider all revenues paid cash.

2012/ Month	Total Revenue	Employees costs	Costs of advertising	Costs of goods	Other Costs	All Costs	Cash flow	Bank Account
Jan.	35 000 €	3 000 €	5 250 €	38 167 €	1 600 €	48 017 €	-13017	40 239 €
Feb.	30 000 €	3 000 €	4 500 €	5 500 €	1 700 €	14 700 €	15 300	55 539 €
March	35 000 €	4 000 €	5 250 €	6 167 €	3 700 €	19 117 €	15 883	71 423 €
April	40 000 €	4 500 €	6 000 €	6 833 €	1 800 €	19 133 €	20 867	92 289 €
May	35 000 €	4 500 €	5 250 €	46 167 €	1 800 €	57 717 €	-22717	69 573 €
June	35 000 €	8 000 €	5 250 €	6 167 €	3 800 €	23 217 €	11 783	81 356 €
July	30 000 €	8 000 €	4 500 €	5 500 €	2 000 €	20 000 €	10 000	91 356 €
August	35 000 €	8 000 €	5 250 €	51 167 €	2 000 €	66 417 €	-31417	59 939 €
Sept.	40 000 €	8 000 €	6 000 €	6 833 €	2 000 €	22 833 €	17 167	77 106 €
Oct.	50 000 €	9 000 €	7 500 €	9 667 €	2 800 €	28 967 €	21 033	98 139 €
Nov.	60 000 €	10 000 €	9 000 €	61 000 €	2 000 €	82 000 €	-22000	76 139 €
Dec.	75 000 €	15 000 €	11 250 €	13 000 €	2 000 €	41 250 €	33 750	109 889 €
Sum	500 000 €	85 000 €	75 000 €	256 167 €	27200€	443 367 €	56 633	x

Other example:

Date	1st	5th	10th	14th	15th
Item	bank account	revenues	employees	warehouse, shop, delivery, accountant	revenues
Amount	$ 5 000	$ 1 500	$ -2 900	$ -3 778	$ 3 000
Status	$ 5 000	$ 6 500	$ 3 600	$ -178	$ 2 822

20th	23rd	25th	30th
IT, telephones	car repair	revenues	revenues
$ -190	$ -400	$ 1 500	$ 2 000
$ 2 632	$ 2 232	$ 3 732	$ 5 732

This example means that on the 14th day you will not be able to pay all your suppliers on time. Your basic options are to raise revenues, which are to be paid on the 5th, to urge your customer to pay in advance, or to call one of your suppliers and inform him of one day postponing the payment. Or you could take credit from your bank. When you are in financial trouble, you still have to **pay yourself first**. Paying yourself first means to take percentage of your income and invest it. Live and pay off your debts only with what is left after investing.

If you pay everyone else first, you will not generate enough pressure to start your inner genius and you will struggle financially. There will be not enough for you if you pay everybody else first. If you pay yourself first and then the people you are indebted to, they will create pressure for you. Pay yourself first anyway. If there is no money in the company's bank account and you have to pay company's bills on time, it can be a hard decision. Sometimes I had to loan my personal money to the company to pay the company's debts on time. I do not recommend that you make the same mistakes as I did. If your company is not generating positive cash for you, it is not a healthy company. You have to make necessary changes in the company to turn it into a money-making machine. If you can't, it is not an asset and you should exit that investment.

If you pay everyone else first and nothing is left for paying you, *what is the reason for you to invest or to do business*? If you don't get what you want from your asset, you will quit sooner or later. The sooner is better. Make paying yourself a first priority and pay everyone else later. Use their pressure to create new income streams and pay them on time, but still pay yourself first. You will find a way to pay them or to get rid of their claims because you will have to. Sometimes you will have to choose whom not to pay on time if there will not be enough money, but you have to still pay yourself first even if you will have bad feelings about this. Let the pressure help you create a solution to this temporary money shortage.

Assets and investing

Assets are something that puts money into your wallet regularly without you having to work. You will need some kind of control mechanism to check if the asset and the people work well. Your job is not an asset. An asset is like if you multiplied yourself and each you (an asset) works for you and sends you a paycheck. The more productive your assets are, the faster you will get rich. Gold and silver are not assets, because until you sell them, they will not put money into your wallet. Every asset has positive cash flow. If it does not have positive cash flow, it is not an asset yet. There are investments that in the beginning have negative cash flow and you have to change that to positive cash flow to make those investments an asset. An example is purchasing rental property, rebuilding it, and renting it after the rebuilding is over. During the time you make reconstructions, you have to pay mortgage, rebuilding costs, real estate taxes and have no rental income, which means you have invested in liability. Only when you change it to positive income will you acquire an asset. You should have some buffer for market changes and control over rental price. If your costs go up, your rental price has to go up also, so that your cash flow from the asset remains stable or it is increased.

Positive income is necessary to get more and more money with every new asset so that you have enough money to purchase the next asset. Without positive income you won't grow your wealth. Positive income is a must. Consider selling your liabilities if they are not generating positive income.

If your assets give you more money than what you spend, it means your personal passive income is higher than your personal spending. You don't need to work to pay your bills anymore. At this point you will be balanced. If your assets generate enough cash flow to cover your spending and still purchase more assets, you are truly rich and financially free. Your assets and money will work for you. You can test this by a simple action – leaving your assets for a year without your interference. When you return to them after a year and your assets grew in real value, your asset reproduction is higher than 1. If you do not increase yours spending, your assets should be able to reproduce themselves.

If you do not have a trustworthy asset manager who will take planning and control of your assets, you will still have to manage your assets. It is good to check your assets personally from time to time, because even a trustworthy manager can forget or make mistakes. Or he can be afraid to tell you the bad news – e.g. that your assets lost or are losing value. The final responsibility will still be on your shoulders.

Professional investors invest with insurance. When you drive your car, you have to have it insured. Investment insurance can be traditional insurance like a contract with insurance company or other insurance means like having a deal giving you control over e.g. bank account of company you invest in. Your insurance begins with exit strategy included in your deal. Exit strategy states how you will get your money back. If you can't protect your asset, you should not buy it. If you don't know how to protect your asset and still want to invest, invest only so much money that you can afford to lose. A little pain and pressure are welcome, because they will allow you to grow your knowledge. You should start with baby steps, then walk and then run. This is good advice for people who don't manage to sustain the loss easily. Don't get emotionally involved in your investment if it is your passive income investment. If you work in the investment, e.g. you are CEO in company you started, emotional involvement is desired. Your passion will help your company to reach the best possible results. If your company is run by someone else, chose a CEO who is passionate about bringing the desired results.

What you should do, when deciding about investment, is to consider what you can lose and what you can gain. What are the probabilities that you will lose or win?

I am the kind of person who takes risks and I have to say I had huge losses. I was sad and I was devastated for some time. I was physically ill. After some time I realized that all I have lost is just money and time. Once I realized what I had learned from the experience it was time to bury the loss and look for new opportunities to earn more money. Don't give up after a few unsuccessful tries. Don't expect that you will win all the time. Learn from the loss and start again. If you earned money before, you can earn it again. You just had valuable and pricy lesson, which cost you money. You have just become a more experienced investor. Think of how can you insure your asset next time and look for new opportunities. There are several types of assets.

Types of assets

Money

Money begets money. When you lend your money to someone and you are paid interest, this money creates new money for you and it becomes your asset. Lending money without receiving interest and collateral is waste of your money and time.

Stocks, bonds, mutual funds

Stocks are paper assets giving you a share of a company. This allows you to take part and vote at shareholders meetings. Stocks are good for cash flow if they pay you a dividend each year. But some companies don't pay dividend at all. Stocks that are not paying dividends are purchased because of potential capital gain. Purchasing stocks for capital gain is gambling if you don't invest with insurance or if you don't have control over the price of the stocks or management of the company.

Bonds are a written promise from the government, a company or other entity that you will get your money back with interest. Not all promises are fulfilled and the issuer of bonds has to be trustworthy. Government bonds are relatively safe investments, as they are almost risk free. But as we saw in Greece, even countries don't keep their promises to pay you your money back. The relative safety of bonds is balanced by low returns in interest rate.

Mutual funds are a collection of stocks and bonds. You are pooling your money with other investors to be able to pay for a professional finance manager who will select specific securities for you.

Alternative Investments

There are alternative investments like Options, Futures, ForEx, Gold, Oil, etc. For the beginning investor I do not recommend starting with investments like this. They are generally high risk/high rewards securities. Good news is that usually you can try trading them on demo accounts without the risk of losing real money. Practice at least for a few months on the demo account and if you prove that you trade profitably with demo money, only then use your real money. Invest your time in education first before you start even with a demo account. I recommend using www.babypips.com/school/ for learning the terminology.

Real estate

Real estate is a piece of land or building. If it puts more money into your pocket than it takes out, it is an asset. Most rich people use real estate to secure their wealth, not to create it. It is better to create your own business which will build or trade the real estate. You will find more info on real estate later in this book.

Businesses

Business that puts money into your pocket without you having to work there is an asset. Business that you have to work in is usually a high paying job plus a possible future asset. Some businesses that were started by owners usually stop their growth or profitability when the owner stops being a CEO. The good news about business is that you can start it with no money and generate very large cash flow. When your company grows profitably and you have a few managers working for you, start to look for the one who will replace you. You should look for your replacement, unless you love your job. Prepare your successor as a leader. When you love your business and your job you created for yourself, it would be foolish to quit - unless someone else can do your work better than you can, which is rare.

Working in your business is almost always financially better than working for someone else, because you are getting a paycheck for your work and you get dividend from yearly profits. If it is not like that even after three years, you should start paying yourself first. If your business is profitable, you can sell it, too. You can't sell your job to someone else. With your own business you have higher control over taxes and you can keep more money for yourself. If you are already rich, you can buy existing business with its managers and as it generates passive income, it becomes your asset. This is the game for the rich. For an average person, it is easier to buy a franchise license with borrowed money and start your own company. Keep in mind that starting your own business means almost no steady paycheck in the beginning and lots of work. There is nothing like working 8 hours a day, five days a week for the beginning businessman. You will have to work a lot more.

Intellectual property

Intellectual property (IP) refers to creations of the mind: inventions, literary or artistic works, symbols, names, images or designs used in commerce. This property needs to generate cash to become an asset. Either one-time cash flow in case you sell your property (like painting, symbol etc.) or regular cash flow in the form of royalties.

An important subject especially connected with IP is its protection. Once your IP is published, it is usually easy to copy. You have to use legal protection like trademarks, protected design, etc. to make it harder for others to use your property.

Investing

Investing is related to saving and deferring consumption with hope of future gain. When you invest, you have to have money, time, risks and profit in your mind.

Look for hidden opportunities before investing. If you know how to change the asset into a more profitable one because of your knowledge, you can turn even a bad investment for one person into great investment for yourself. If you can negotiate a better interest rate, prolong payment time, lower monthly payments, and change negative cash flow into positive cash flow, do it.

There will be investments you have to let go if you want to keep sleeping soundly. For example, if the company management is weak and you are not able to replace it. Good management should discuss problems with you, inform you and you should see their enthusiasm towards solving problems. Be cautious if you see them hiding problems.

Peter Lynch, one of the great investors, has said that the "*key organ for investing is the stomach, not the brain*". In other words, you need to know how much volatility you can stand to see in your investments. You've taken on too much risk when you can't sleep at night because you are worrying about your investments. First you have to experience investments where you will not be able to sleep well to find out where the end of your comfort zone is. Then, you can expand your comfort zone with more gained experience in investing and learn how to change the investments in a way that will allow you to sleep well again.

When you invest, you will have to know the numbers and the facts. Due diligence is used to separate facts from opinions which are presented to you as the facts. You have to recognize what are facts and what is just seller's wish to be facts.

Don't go with the crowd if you are looking for great investments. Crowds go to good investments too late and they pay too much. Greatest investors like Soros or Buffet buy assets when everybody else is selling because they want to get them as cheap as possible. When ordinary people, who are not investors, start to invest in certain stocks, it's time for you to sell at profitable price. Soon the stocks will rise in a bubble and then they will collapse. Look for assets that are not popular at that time, but offer good cash flow. Buy when the market is low and sell when the market is high. This is basic rule of trade whatever you trade with – buy cheap, sell at high price. Opposite to common belief, it is easier to find good investments when the market is low than when the market is high. Profit is made when you buy. This means that the day you become the owner, you could sell it for more than you paid for it. You are profitable from the beginning. You need to buy undervalued assets, not average or overvalued assets and hope for their further rise of value.

Great investments are found when the seller needs money quickly and is desperate to sell. Be careful though as the con men can sell you something fake at a low price telling you that they are in great need for the money and that's why they are selling so low. You have to do due diligence and separate facts from fiction. You will be told both. If the seller is pushy and you don't have enough time for doing due diligence, leave it. The only thing you can do quickly with your money is to lose it.

If you are a beginning investor who is looking for average investments, you can go with the average crowd. You should invest only in assets you understand. Average investments with minimal risks caused by lack of knowledge are O.K. at the beginning of your investor's career. As you evolve and get more knowledge and experience, you can move towards more profitable investments.

Always, I mean always, when you take risk or debt on yourself, you have to make profit on it. Don't lend money interest free to your friends unless you are meaning it as a gift to them. Lend only against solid assets, such as real estate, and with a signed deal prepared by good lawyer. Use valuable items, which you will store as collateral until you get your money back. It would be best not to lend money to friends at all. There is old saying **Lend money only to a person, who you don't want to see again**. I have a friend who once came to me and told me about his business idea and wanted to borrow 5000 €, because he was declined by the bank. I knew him since my childhood and the business idea had economic sense, so I did it. Unfortunately he did not start the business and thus he made no profit. When the payment date came, he asked for prolongation and refused to pay as we agreed in our contract. I had to use a debt collector to get the money. In the end I received the money back, but it was not a pleasant experience. It is better not to lend money to friends or family. You can lose that friend or money very easily.

Ways to get rich

The surest way how to get rich is by running your successful business. It is not the easiest way, but it is the surest and proven way. Fortunately creating a business is not easy and you need lots of courage to start creating one and lots of brains to make it a success. These prerequisites weed out the 95% of people from your competition because you are among the bold and determined winning 5% person.

I will not bullshit you - running a business is hard way to earn money. Don't count on regular working hours or on regular paychecks. It is hard, but rewarding and still, it is the surest way to get rich. And the good news is the longer you run a business and the more experience you will get, the easier it becomes. Many of today's so called successful businessmen have a record of unsuccessful business behind them – it is natural part of running a business – trial and error, trial and error and then trial and then bang – finally a success.

It may be easier to get rich by investing, but you need a lot of money and experience to invest wisely. And in reality if you are not rich already, there are not many ways to you can get your hands on capital big enough to invest and make yourself richer. If you have a proven record of being a good investor, then you may be able to persuade people with money to give you their money under control and invest for them and share the profits. But you have to have this success record with you first.

Investing in real estate is usually a way of securing your riches. If you are not a real estate developer (a businessman building and selling the real estate), your chances of becoming rich by buying and selling real estate is low. First create the capital with your business and then you can invest it in real estate. Not the opposite way. Business is the surest way to create that capital which will make you rich later. This is why the biggest part of this book is focusing on creating and running a successful business.

Business owner

If you choose to start your own business as your way to wealth, you have chosen the hardest, but possibly the most rewarding, way. As a successful business owner you will have to experience emotional and financial highs and lows. There will be good times and there will be bad times. Running a fulltime business requires lots of skills in various areas. You will have to deal with hard decisions, handle pressure from other people and work overtime for few years. Your time and energy will be repaid if your company is successful and generates excessive cash flow for you covering all your needs. If you turn that company into an asset by having others to manage and work there, you will be financially free.

To face the facts, you have to know risks of starting your own company. Most startup companies fail. Lack of experience, planning, investment capital, poor inventory management, over-investment in fixed assets, poor credit management, unexpected growth, competition, and low sales all take their toll. I hope you will be among those who succeed. But even if you fail, there is no better way to gain business experience than running your own business. You will gain invaluable experience even if you fail at your first company. Learn what you did wrong, correct the mistakes and start your second company.

If your losses were so heavy that you don't want to do start a business ever again, no problem. By experiencing your own business, you can use that knowledge in analyzing other investments. I think that your time spent on building your own company is time well spent and probably there is no training program where you could learn more and get that experience into your blood.

Taking risks and adversity is a natural part of running a business. If you don't feel like you are able to accept high risks and loses, you can start a franchise company. Your franchisor will give you manual how to build your own successful business without beginners mistakes. The difficult part with the franchise is that you need starting capital to purchase a franchise license.

Another quite safe way to learn to run your own business is to build a multilevel network business. The costs are very low and you will have to learn how to sell, how to manage people, and how to handle rejections.

For increasing your businesses results you have to focus on testing, measuring and creating the business system. If you innovate something, you have to test it to see if it brings better results. Don't blindly accept that new marketing activity is profitable just because your marketing agency told you so, or because all others do it and it is cool. Unless the new activity measurably brings you more money, being only cool is not cool. There are lots of companies who went bankrupt because they spent a large amount of money on branding, which was like throwing money out of the window. There are lots of companies who have very creative advertisements, which were awarded in advertisement competitions, but running those ads was not profitable for them. Ask yourself if you want your marketing agency to win marketing competitions because of the ad for your product or you want the sales increased profitably for the money invested.

We have tried Facebook advertisements multiple times and we have measured them. It was never profitable. It was cool to have those ads, but it was a waste of money. Maybe it works for some other companies, but it did not work for us. We had an increase in the number of visitors, but as we sell online, it is not our goal to have lots of visitors, but to have lots of customers. **Marketing which does not increase sales profitably is wrong marketing.** This is true even if your marketing agency tells you otherwise. Brand recognition won't pay your bills. Increased sales and profits will. Remember - you have to test all new activities, measure them and put them into your system if proven to work well for you. We had good results with AdWords and our e-mailing database campaigns.

The company system must be result oriented and it must bring good results independent of people operating it. The system gives rules and limits to people and if they operate under these rules, they will have good results whether they like it or not. That's why franchise companies are successful – they use proven systems.

When you are creating a business, it should not be about creating a product, but about creating a system. Products come and go with their life cycle. What successful businessmen advice is to never give up an idea of creating a company, which will last. If you don't give up and optimize your company all the time, you will win in the end. Create a company, which is great place to work at, and which has great system creating great products. Your task as a businessman is to create such a place and let your employees create great products.

Business is a team sport. A single person does not have much chance against a well-organized teams of people. You have to create a team of people with common goals as soon as possible. When creating your winning team, look for people who exhibit the needed skills for their work and are also trustworthy, brave, responsible, respectful and honest.

Market, marketing and SALES

There are hundreds books on marketing and sales theory and there is not enough space to cover everything in this book. We will focus the on practical parts of marketing and sales and I will try to make the theory short and simple.

Marketing is a very simple process: You bring value to the marketplace and someone who wants to get what you have will trade his value (usually the money) for your value (usually a product). Value is subject and time specific. If I have enough water, I am not willing to pay for another bottle. I (subject) don't feel the need for water at **this** particular time because I have all the water I need **right now**. If you would offer to sell me a bottle of water next week and I had none, it would be invaluable to me. Needs and desires change in time just like the ability to buy. I can be in need of water, I can desire it, but I do not have enough money to buy it right now.

That is what salesmen have to understand when they are rejected. Rejection means just that this specific person is not interested in your specific product at that particular time. He can reject you today and buy thousands of products next week.

People solve their most appealing problems first and forget the other problems until the biggest appealing problem is solved.

Emotions are the main reason why we buy. Sales are about emotions. If you know how to spark desire in your potential customer, you win. If your potential customer wants your product, he will find some rational argument why he needs it. Have him sign the contract while his emotions are high. People buy for various reasons – search online for "100 reasons why people buy". People are not buying your products; they are buying solutions to their problems. People don't buy cars like Porsche or Ferrari because they need a car. They already have multiple cars. What they want is increased feeling of self-confidence or feeling of being successful when they are seen with their car.

You can create your business and products designed for desperate people around their misfortune. There aren't many authors who will tell you that you can build your best business around desperate people. Their bad luck can be your profit. Desperate people are often in great need and if they have enough of money, they can be your best customers. They can pay you before something bad happens in form of insurance. It can be illness, disasters, job loss, retirement care, etc. or they can pay you after something happens to them – house repair, coffin, or wreath production, etc. How do those businesses work? Customers pay you money and you give them **a promise** that if something they insured happens, you will take care of them based on the contract.

You can create your business or products about peoples' happiness too. Happy people are also good customers because they are driven by emotions. Valentine's Day is a good business day. You can produce nice hearts in China and sell them for a ten times higher price in US or Europe. After paying transport, duties and taxes, marketing and logistics, you can still have nice profit.

Marketing tips

Don't be afraid to coordinate your marketing with others – you can add your partner's product or discount for his product to your contact database you are sending (online or by post) and he will do the same. The best partners are those who supply complementary products to yours.

Learn copywriting. It is really worth it. In combination with testing and measuring you will increase your sales after finding the combination of "magic words" which trigger purchasing decision with your customers. Most common "magic words" are sale, limited offer, discount, etc.

Lots of people search for product reviews online before they choose to buy. Use your expertise and give free tips which are related to your products and don't forget to insert links to your web page.

Sales always go first

You have to learn how to sell even if you are not running a business. It is not as difficult because we all are born sellers. Small kids are salespersons if they want something from you.

You can have the best brand recognition in the

world, millions of people can like your brand, but if you don't receive money from your customer, you will go bankrupt. Taking an order is not the same as the sale. Taking an order is just a promise that your potential customer will pay for your goods or service. Until you hold that money, it is just a promise, nothing more. This is mainly true in business-to-business operations, where money exchange is postponed to goods or service delivery. Until you have past experience with the customer, always take significant deposit. A customer who does not have money to pay a deposit is probably not a trustworthy customer.

Effective selling is both science and art. You have to test various scripts or approaches (art) and measure results (science) to see which brings the best one. Each word has a smaller or bigger effect on the sale, so choose the words and their order carefully and then test them. After finding the most effective scheme, use it and stick to it. I have learned that the **creativity kills sales**. The right words trigger the right emotions in your prospect and the sale is about emotions.

Sale text must sell a solution to customer's problem by creating an emotional response. Only after a successful emotional response comes reasoning and rationalization of those emotions. Emotions always win over reasons.

When you sell, don't let your ego manage your actions or feelings. If a customer refuses to buy, it can be your product he refuses or it can be you – if he does not want to do business with you, because of lack of sympathy or trust. You have to find out what was the real reason behind the refusal. There are not many people who will tell you directly that they don't like you. If you are the reason for refusal, work on your behavior and mindset and then try it with the next prospect.

As a sales person you have to accept challenges and hostile environment. Once you decide to face the challenge, think about the desired result of your activity, and see your goal and reward. If you think about quitting, think once more about the reward. Is it worth your trouble? If yes, continue and don't give up.

If the reward is not worth your trouble, probably your goal is too small. Dream and think big! What will be worth of your trouble? There will be problems to solve in everything you do and with bigger problems solved, the bigger person you will become. You will solve a big problem a few times and the big problem will become small or insignificant to you. You have to face the challenge. Do what you fear to do. Got it?

I was afraid to make phone calls and talk to people when I was younger. A few days in call center changed that. It was hard but I got used to it and now it is no problem at all to call somebody and ask what I want from him. Training, repetition and experience will help you to overcome any problem. You have to train and practice to get more skills.

Prepare mentally for bad days. You can be sure they will come. It is not the days that go smooth that grow your character. It is the days where Mr. Murphy and his laws pay you a visit that shapes your character. If you do everything right and the goal was not reached, then it was not your fault. As a salesman you will face lot of adversity and refusals. Don't take it personally. If you know you have done what you should do, throw the refusal with negative feelings away quickly. Don't let it ruin your good attitude. There are things you can't influence. Maybe your customer had a bad day. Don't give up. Forget that experience and focus on your goal and reward. It is natural to fail a few times before you reach your goal. Throw that negative thought about what happened away - don't analyze it too long. It can hurt you.

Focus on what you want right now. Fill your mind with that single intention. There is nothing else in your mind, just that single intention. No past blame or shame, no worry how you will look like or feel like. You will get what you want sooner or later. Don't waste your time by *trying* to get it. Feel that you are already getting it. There is no past and no future. There is just now, you and your intention.

Push all negative feeling and thoughts out of your mind by putting positive feelings and thoughts inside. Place positive thoughts into your mind like: *"My next customer will make big order, because my offer is so good and suitable for his needs."* Reward yourself even for positive attitude and for positive actions you took. Give yourself applause for not quitting and call the next potential customer. You deserve it. Think of your past successes and keep that mindset that you had when you succeeded.

Handling refusal is a very important skill in your transformation from zero to hero. You simply can't make everybody like you or the product you offer and you can't sell anything to anyone. Some people will buy and some will not. Get used to it. Your job is to find those who will.

If you want to get rid of negative emotions, follow three steps.

1. Ask yourself honestly what really bothers you? Be specific. If it is something that another person does, ask yourself if it really bothers you or if you are just bored and you want to skirmish.

2. Stop your inner speech, which is blaming everyone, including yourself, and stop your negative emotions. Our mind has limited capacity for emotions. If you focus on positive emotions, your negative emotions have to leave. There is not enough space for them. Make yourself busy. When you are busy doing the important stuff, there is no space for self-blame or blaming others. There is just you, now, and taking action at the present time. Don't be afraid of the future. Prepare for it but don't be afraid of it. You will manage somehow.

3. Practice *empty mind* technique to stop your inner voice for a while. It will help you to stay focused.

Refusals and objections are normal and they are not the problem. Your negative reaction to the refusal is the problem. Don't take refusal or objection personally. Keep your head and emotions clear as much as possible, because only a clear head will help you to find the right answer to the objection or refusal. If the prospect does not want to buy, it means nothing more than that he is not willing to buy this product at the present time. Maybe your offer is so good, that he thinks your offer cannot be realistic. Ask him under which conditions is he prepared to buy.

If you face many refusals in one line, take a break and call some of your happy customers. Ask them how they are satisfied with your product. It will help you to keep your motivation high. If it didn't help, take a break and go for a run or walk. Exercise until your hormones are released to your blood and you have a good feeling about yourself. Do your favorite sport and beat your personal record.

In sales it is the same as in sports. Keep your energy high and focus on reaching the goal. Work at 100% of your effort level. Getting used to beating your competition in sports will help you to get used to beating your competition in business.

Be your own customer. Purchase your products in mystery shopping from time to time to see what your customer sees. Call your company under different names and write down how long you had to wait and if the person who picked up your call was competent to answer your questions or solve your problem. Take your time and compare your offer with your competitors' offers. Ask for offers from your competitors. If they use easier ways for you as a customer to buy, copy it. Customers can be lazy, so make it as easy as possible for them to buy from you.

Customer types

There are three main types of customers:
1. VIP customers are those who make the biggest profit for your company and you need to treat them well to keep them. If you lose your VIP customer, it will be felt on sales significantly.
2. Regular customers are those who buy from you from time to time and their orders are average. If you lose them, it is not such a big deal.
3. Customers to fire are those who make your

company experience a loss. Usually they require discounts and then make lots of complaints. The best solution I could figure out so far is to politely direct them to your competition.

With the first two customer types you have to make them repetitive offers. If they bought once, they can buy again. Customers you already have, are the company's treasure. I read in a book of one marketing guru that costs for converting new customer to customer are eight times higher than with your existing customer. From my experience it is truth. Use your customer database and give them special offers.

How to handle objections - theory

You have to have 4 things in mind when customer tells his objections:

- What customer said
- What we have heard
- How do we interpret what we have heard
- What customer really had in his mind

Example: Customer said that he needs more time to think about your offer. If there were no noises, you have heard that the customer needs more time to think about your offer. You interpret it like the customer is not attracted to your offer. What the customer really had in mind we can just guess. Maybe he is tired and wants to postpone calculation of your offer to the next day or he wants to ask your competitor for his offer and take time to compare your offers. Or he expects a bribe from you. It can be anything.

With study and experience you will find out what to do to get the customer order and pay for your product. Objections need to be examined and explained. Never wrangle with the customer and never speak scornfully about his objections. Answer them shortly with confidence. If you don't know the answer, make a promise to find it out and give the answer later. Don't be negative about contacting the customer again and again. There is nothing bad about contacting him if you want to help him.

How to handle objections – what really works

My friend who is successful salesman handles objections easily. He smiles and promises his future customer what he wants to hear. If customer asks for delivery of heavy machinery, which is twice above my friends' company's capacity, he has no problem and promises they will deliver it. Then he pushes everyone in the company to make production as high as possible and if necessary he contacts the competition for help to get additional production. If they can deliver, then it is a huge success and he is the company's star. If they can't deliver everything, it is still a huge success as he managed to fill their capacity over 100%. The customer usually really needs what was produced ASAP, so he pays for it to get what is already produced and waits for the rest of the delivery.

In my friend's opinion, it is better to have a "one time customer" than to have none. And he is right! I am too honest of a salesman and I don't give promises I am not sure I can fulfill, but I have to admit my friend is better salesman than I am. It is money that matters in business. If you can't deliver what you promised, you can still explain that you had some problems at the factory and put blame on someone else. You will keep a good personal relationship with your customer because of some gifts like expensive wine or other alcohol or money. I didn't like it, but it works.

Bribes worked, work, and will work. For some people (usually small contracts) alcohol, tickets, and holidays work the best as this is more considered a gift than a bribe and for some people (high decision makers for large contracts) a percentage of the contract as a bribe works the best. It is better to start with gifts to build a relationship before you move to financial bribes. There is a small chance that person you give your present or bribe to will report you. If you are afraid how the person will react, start with small gifts. Bribes are illegal in most countries and I do not recommend you to do it. It is your decision and your responsibility if you bribe. It can be illegal even if it is a common practice – we can use as an example the representatives of pharmaceutical companies bribing doctors to prescribe their products. It is common practice, but I have seen a representative who was reported to the police by one doctor.

A second example of very good salesman is my former partner of our first company. His definition of salesman is to promise you what you need to hear, get you to sign the order, and then deliver what is possible to deliver. If he manages to deliver 50% of what he promised, he thinks it is a success. It is your problem if you did not put some penalties for late or partial delivery to the contract, you should be smarter. I have to admit this approach works for him well.

Art of negotiation – learn how to say yes and no

When you negotiate, you have to decide if the person you negotiate with is trustworthy, and if he and the company he represents will deliver what he promises. There are two kinds of business relationships 1. long-term and 2.short-term. If you are going to have a long-term business relationship I advise you to seek win-win deals. However, be careful, because your partner can tell you that he also seeks a long term relationship and that he represents a great company with long history, but in reality he is there to squeeze you out of as much money as possible to get his bonus before he quits his job at his company. The more he speaks about how important their company is and the more he plays "the theatre", the more you should be careful. Don't have bad feelings about checking for yourself how much of what he said is truth and what his company can deliver in reality.

When you both seek short-term business, you better be prepared for a hard negotiation where your partner wants to win over you by being dramatic. He will take any advantage he can. That's why one time business like selling a house can be so confrontational. Don't expect those actors to give you something back for your concession. If you fall back, he will see it as your weak point and he will take advantage of it with great pride.

Learn to say no.

You have to learn and experience not to have bad feeling about saying no, even if other people will try to make you feel so. You are responsible only for yourself and your family. You are not responsible for helping other people. Mostly they won't help you if you switched positions – even if they say they would. Bad people will push you to help them and demand your help. Treat yourself with respect and stop being misused. Helping someone does not mean you will do all the work for him. This would be short-term help. You can help people by coaching them, however. Allow them to grow. Don't do the hard work for them.

When in doubt, ask for more time to decide. If they push, say no. Let your brain think it out thoroughly while you sleep and then listen to your gut. When you feel bad about a deal even if you have no particular reason, wait. The world is full of opportunities and as one opportunity vanishes, a new one emerges.

Make a lot of offers when selling and get lot of offers when purchasing something. There are BIG price differences in offers from different suppliers. When we needed to inspect our supplier and get basic information on our Chinese producer's credibility we were offered a price for the inspection from one company 2.000 € and from the other 320 €. The first was Czech and the second was from Hong Kong. The report from the Czech company was 3 pages of text with low informational value and the second report from AsiaInspection.com had very detailed information - 30 page PDF even with photographs of the real inspectors and the company.

With whom to do and not to do business

Understand that some people will tell you whatever they think you need to hear to do what they want you to do – they won't have a bad feeling about this – they consider it normal. Actually they will think it is your fault when you believe what they tell you. Once my ex-business partner told me after I found out that he lied to me persistently that it is my mistake I believed him - "You should have known it is not realistic what I told you and it can't be done." was his reply.

After very long time I have to admit he was right – I should have known that a person who is a liar will lie to me. Some people are liars and when you find out that they lie to other people, you can be sure they will lie also to you. They have no bad feelings about this. Why should they? For them, you and "some other person" are the same. Do not get me wrong – it is not just the bad crooks who lie – sometimes they can be even your friends who don't want to make you sad and they will tell you something they expect you want to hear – e.g. they promise you they will do something and after you leave, they forget their promise with no bad feeling at all.

You can't change a liar – he is and he will be a liar. Don't waste your time trying to change him by being honest and good to him. He won't change. What you can do is learn how to separate people whose promise has a value and they are ready to bring sacrifice to fulfill their promises. Learn how to recognize people who do not feel they are bound by their word if it does not suit them. With experience, you will recognize the second group easier because they have similar talk patterns, e.g. they speak about their superior experience and expertise, and how they never failed in the long term and most of all how you can trust them. It is because they know they have to create trust, and their mind will be occupied with questions if you already trust them and if they can put their offer on the table. They will play theatre, tell you "fairytales" they prepared in advance and when they are convinced it is the right time, they will make you an offer. Usually, if they consider you smart or an equal partner, they expect you not to accept the first offer and expect you to try to negotiate better conditions. That is the reason they give you, let's say a 25% less favorable price than they are willing to accept because they keep their space for negotiation. Negotiation is a game to them and you should play by the rules of the game. Rules of the game can differ, but some rules I experienced so far are:

- If you can't enforce your partner to deliver his promises, then promises will be all you will have in the end. Lawsuits are costly and do take months or years to finish. Avoid them if there is quicker and more profitable way to solve the problem.

- If there is no penalty for late payment, expect your partner to pay later than agreed.

- Your partner can legally force you to fulfill your part of the agreement even if he is breaking his part. You have to check your contract with a good lawyer before you sign. Compare the costs of a lawyer with the costs of what you can lose.

- Don't take partners into your business if you haven't spent enough time with them to find out if they are honest people and you can trust them. Sometimes you will break this rule and you may be lucky to end up having a good partner, but sometimes you won't. Be prepared by having a clause in your contract how to end your business relationship if it does not work.

On breaking promises

I wanted to sell a share of my company in exchange for passive cash flow from the buyer. We had an oral agreement, but the transaction was not signed in the end. I was not surprised because I experienced the same behavior from my friend John at college and later from my business partner. Experience helps you to avoid naivety and disappointment, which is often later followed by the anger. The buyer changed his mind and he had the full right to do so. Before the contract is signed, you can change anything. It reminded me of how I sold my best friend a guitar during college. We agreed that he would pay me later and he took the guitar home. After two weeks I asked him to give me my money, but he gave me my guitar back. He had unexpected costs because of the dentist so he said he could not afford the guitar anymore.

Lesson learned: *It is said that the only money you can count on is that in your pocket. But remember there are thieves around, so the only money you can really count on is the money you already spent.* ***Always take money up front.***

Bonus tip: *When other people break their promises given to you, you don't have to fulfill your promises given to them.*

Managing people

Managing people takes lot of discipline. As a manager and a leader you have to be respected and trusted. Otherwise you will be shot in the back.

People expect you to be their example and to be able to do everything you expect them to do. Of course you don't have to know how to do everything, but you must be able to give direction when your employees come to you and ask how to do it. You don't have to understand all the specific tasks of your subordinate, as he is the one who is being paid to know the details. You need to know the basic guidelines for given task – where to look or whom to call for the correct answer. What you have to know is how to check results of your subordinates and have the authority to reward them for good results just like you have the authority to punish them for bad results.

Every time you agree on something with your employees, take written note of the agreement – it can be an e-mail for example. Your memory is not your best friend while studying, as we tend to remember what we want in a way that we want to remember. Written agreements are mandatory. The best way I have figured it so far are operations manuals, where person can read what he should do, how should he do it, and most of all, why it is important to do it and what effects will it have if he does it good or does it wrong. Minimal, standard and maximal qualities of the work done helps you to be objective at monthly, one to one, evaluations of reached results. Results oriented goals, rewards, and punishments are welcome. Rewarding and punishing people by measurable results takes a lot of managing burden from your shoulders and makes it easier at performance evaluation meetings to give feedback.

What I found to work best is to take notes for this evaluation meeting during the whole month, not just before the meeting. On a separate sheet with responsibilities, goals, and tasks for specific employee, write down deadlines for each task and as the month goes, write down newly appointed and agreed on tasks, mark down fulfilled tasks and comment it if there is reason for it. At the meeting I just review the sheet and send it to person by e-mail, give feedback to person, and based on results, I tell what is the reward or punishment for reached results. Then we talk about possible ways to improve the performance of the person, of the company or of my management. Example:

Task	Priority	Deadline	Status	Comment
Invoicing orders and shipping them to customers.	High	Daily	Done	Good Work.
Keeping office clean	Low	Weekly	Failed	On 14th May there was dirt on the floor.

> **Notes:** This month there were lots of orders, I liked the speed at which you fulfilled them. It is necessary to call our customers and offer them cross sells – remember, you are getting a bonus from cross sells.

During the month, give feedback immediately if something is done very good or not according to the standards. Then take notes on the performance sheet, so that you won't forget it by the end of the month at the performance review meeting.

Sometimes it is difficult to give negative feedback to people you like, but as a manager you have to do it. Always give feedback just for the performance, not for the person itself. Judge your words before you tell them. It's a good habit to write the performance report in advance, re-read it to check if you use the right words, and then tell it to person. After giving and receiving feedback, write down agreed tasks for next month, put it together with the past report, and e-mail it to the person. If something is not written, it will be forgotten.

Expecting the best of yourself and others is motivational. However you and the others are just normal people with weaknesses and we all make mistakes. If the mistake was reprimanded and is done again, you with your subordinate have to face consequences. Have written limits on what to tolerate and what is a reason to fire a person. Be specific in those limits. Just stating that your employee is slow will not work well enough. Use sentences like "Missing deadline for tax declaration by four days." Let your people know the rules in advance. If employees do not obey the basic game rules (even if they say they do), fire them. Sometimes your subordinate will tell you that everything is done, that he finished assigned task just to get rid of you. You have to know whose of your people are to be trusted just by their word and whose have to be checked regularly with punishment for lying to you.

Face the fact that almost all your co-workers will try to fool you. Get used to it. It is normal and you have to expect that. You can't trust most of them for 100%. What you can do is to prepare your company system in a way, where they will not be able to really abuse you. They will copy your company and try to start their own. It is normal. It will happen.

If you see your team as a group of good fighters, don't micro-manage them and don't put bureaucracy on top of their activities. If you have to manage your people a lot, they are not the right people in the right place. Everybody makes hiring mistakes and you will also to it. You realize it when you have to spend too much of your time managing your people. The better the results people have, the less you have to manage them. If they underperform and you have to manage them often, look for a replacement.

Hiring and keeping the right people

Hiring the right person is the most important step in managing the person. You need to know exactly what is expected of each employee including values, attitude, experience, and skills. Candidates need to be informed of business culture, key goals and key measures by which the employee will be evaluated and the purpose of the work that needs to be done. You have to identify if a candidate is suitable for the position and what feelings does he have toward implementing the purpose behind the position.

At the interview you have to find out his real skills, as some of the candidates lie in their CV or they just can't evaluate the level of their skills realistically. For long term and key positions, basic values of the candidate play a more important factor than his skills, which can be learned. You have to create a picture of his character, work ethics, base intelligence, ambitions, dedication to fulfill his commitments, and his basic values. You want to know what kind of person he is, not just what skills he has. To find out, ask questions about their important decisions in their life. This will help you to look into their basic values.

When you know that the person has necessary character, values, and skills, you still have to find out if he is suitable for the team and, most of all, if he will be compatible with his direct manager. Their relation is critically important.

When a company grows its operations, you need more people and if you still haven't found the right person for the position, you will be tempted to hire an incompetent person for the job. I should tell you "Don't do it, it will be a mistake." but you will do it anyway. You simply need one more person to fill empty place in your company machine to operate correctly and you will take your chances that the person will adapt well. When you have to do this, be honest with yourself, because you can offer only a temporary job until you find the competent person.

The best way would be to hire services from a company until you have found the right employee. Or maybe you will find out that your supplier is more effective and you can outsource this position. When the person is looking for a stable job and you inform him it is only temporary, you will probably demotivate him quite a lot and you can face low performance with the person and later also with people who had good performance, but under a new colleague's influence, their performance dropped too. What you can do to increase it is to give him ambitious goals and if he reaches them, he will be offered a stable job. If he considers the goals unreachable, it will still demotivate him, however, so keep the goals realistic.

Beware of "rotten apple" employees. They are those who do not meet standard behavior expected in your organization. Other employees, when seeing him doing a bad job and still managing to stay on board, will be influenced and demotivated. Why should they try hard if someone else is underperforming and still receives his paycheck? If you keep the rotten apple in a bin with other healthy apples, what will happen? ... other apples will start to rot as well. In this situation you have to be quick and remove the rotten apple. Otherwise you can lose the whole apple bin.

Everyone working for you is expected to do his tasks the best as he possibly can do. With more time spent on his position, he is expected to be more and more productive. If his productivity is not growing, he should leave that position or your team. This is very easy to write, but very difficult to implement most of the times, because of our emotions and good relationship with the employees.

When hiring, managers are choosing the best person that is currently available on the market and the best person available still doesn't have to be the right person. Until you hire and test him, you can't know for sure if he is the one. It is a trial and error process – you hire him and you will see his performance. If he is good he stays, if he is not, he leaves. Modern intelligence tests help a lot to find out what kind of character is applying for the position and if he has needed character traits. Look for responsible people who are willing to obey system rules and are oriented for best possible results. The best companies have systems that enable employees to produce sustainable results. Creative people with a lack of discipline can have a problem fitting into your company system.

One approach is to think of the job as a role playing game. Employee starts as novice player and with each level of experience and skills increase produces better results. Those better results have to be measurable and you as a manager have to show the employee what progress he has made. With each level of experience gained in measured results an employee goes up in benefits and prestige. It is like in karate – you start with white belt and when you prove yourself to be worthy of next level, you pass the test and you are given next belt.

What is **extremely necessary** for an employee is **to see the progress** and to know, that you (as an employer) are going the right direction. For ambitious people it is better to be in a worse starting point and know it will get better (that you will reach next level and you will move forward), than to be in a good position and know it is going nowhere (you are comfortable now, but this is the final stop, there is nowhere to go to make it better and your only option is to leave the company to keep growing).

You can't motivate people as a manager. They either have the motivation inside or they don't. What you as a manager can do is to eliminate demotivators. Once the person is motivated to do the work, the biggest influence on demotivation is the direct manager and money. Removing money as a demotivator is easy - connect performance with financial rewards. If person does all the quality work that he was hired for, he gets a fixed amount of money. If he wants more money, he has to deliver higher performance. Have this reward system checked multiple times and make sure it is profitable for the company. Once you have the reward system ready, sign the system with your employee and your questions of pay raises is solved. If he wants more money, he has to increase agreed on measurable results.

Direct management has to understand what is important in the work of his subordinates, he has to lead, manage and play fair.

A very good text written on management that I recommend you to read is _The One Minute Manager by Blanchard & Johnson_. This book explains principles of good hiring, as well as effective and timesaving management.

The best managers speak and spend their time with each of their subordinates. They find out what his dreams are, what his strong and weak parts are, and what his goals are. They work carefully with each of them and take notes about their decisions, behavior, and actions. They take their time to study the people. They also note the desires of their subordinates from themselves. Some people want to be led and managed more often, and some don't. Ask them how often they do want to receive feedback from you, what their goals are, where they see themselves in 5 years, and what was their biggest recognition and what they received it for. After their study is over, divide your people into those who are to be kept and those who have to leave. Once the decision is made, act quickly.

The best managers make a list of people working for them and sequence them according to their productivity with the best on the top. Then they make a list of people of whom they spend their time with and how much time they spent with them. The best managers spend most of the time with their best people and they give them the most rewards. It is natural.

Being fair does not mean to behave the same way to everybody, but behave the way the person deserves to be treated based on his performance and behavior. This gives a clear signal to your subordinates that the better results they will have, the more support they will get.

The best managers ask 2 questions when making decisions about the future of an employee: 1. Is the person with poor performance easily trainable? 2. Does he have bad performance because of his direct superior? If the answer is "no" to both questions, the person lacks necessary talent and he needs to be placed somewhere else. It is the manager's responsibility to put that person in a place where he will be successful - whether the employee likes it or not. If you don't have proper and open position for that person in your company, fire him. You can give him advice, what position you think he will be suitable for his personality and talents.

25 free tips on hiring and managing people

- If you have doubts about the person when you hire him, don't hire. You will solve many future problems if you keep this advice.

- Remember that the person working for you is not there to be your friend, but to earn the money. Do not expect any gratitude or loyalty for giving this person a secure paycheck.

- Don't hire your friends or family members. It WILL be hard for you to fire them when they underperform. I would hire only one or two of my relatives, because I know them for years and their work ethics is that great, that I would take the risk.

- Once you know that you need to make change in human resources, do it quickly, don't lose time. Before you fire someone, find out if he is the right person for some other position in your company.

- Good employees have results. Bad employees have excuses. Fire the bad ones ASAP.

- Write down specific results you want your employee to achieve and who is responsible for the results. I will give you the example of an operation manual, which has necessary specifications for job position. Such a manual should be given to the employee first day in his new job and he should sign that he read it and will work according to it.

- Put your best people on the biggest opportunities, not on the biggest problems.

- Train your people for success from the beginning. Don't start to train them only after they make their first error. Start training them immediately. Remind them of the expected performance and goals. Be specific.

- Once the mistake is done by your employee, you both have to admit it and correct it. The employee has to understand what went wrong, why it went wrong, and how to do it well the next time.

- Expect more and more of your people. They will adjust to your expectations.

- Subordinates watch their superior carefully and soon they know everything about him. They want to believe him and they usually will, until he gives them reason why not to believe him. If you are a manager, be sure that you are being watched for your mistakes just like for what you do right. Be an example for them, as they will mimic your behavior.

- Keep work relationships professional. You are their manager and a leader. Camaraderie is usually not the right approach. Your first goal is to reach planned company results, then the results you agreed on with your team and only then there are goals of individual team member to be reached. You all are paid to deliver results for the company. You can be friends in your free time.

- Once the person is hired and you as his supervisor are evaluating his performance, one critical question will help you – *"If I was to hire the person again to this position, would I do it?"* and if your answer is anything else than yes, there was a hiring mistake. One more question can help you if you feel bad about firing the person *"If this person comes to me and tells me that he found a new job and he is leaving, would I feel disappointed or would I feel relieved?"*

- If a mistake is done by your employee, tell him quickly and tell him face to face to protect his dignity. That does not apply for repeated mistakes. Describe the mistake and let the responsible person correct it. Don't let the anger within you grow without telling the responsible person about his mistakes, as it will ruin your relationship. Be quick and be honest. If you will not tell him, your expectations of his performance will drop in your mind and soon also in his real performance will drop as well. You have to give him feedback even if it is hard for you.

- Set realistic and ambitious goals. Performance and productivity must grow. People need to see the better future.

- Expect both you and your employees to perform better and better until you are the best in the world.

- A manager has to spend most of his time with his best people, not with the weakest.

- Inform your people about future plans. It helps them to be loyal, because you show them they are part of the company and you count on them in the future.

- Be watchful. Catch people doing something right and give them approval. People need to hear how their good performance is valued.

- Ask the responsible person what is going on when his performance drops or increases. They expect to be monitored and managed.

- Don't play games with your people. Let them know how they stand with you. If they perform well, tell them. If they perform bad, tell them too and tell them what performance is expected from them. Information has to flow from you to them and from them to you. Write performance reports and discuss it with them. Look for solutions on how to increase productivity and performance - both theirs and yours. A lack of information from your side can be interpreted as lack of your trust. If you will not tell them about future plans of the company, they will believe gossips they heard and the gossip can be far from the truth.

- Meetings – prepare agendas of meeting in advance and start on time. Start on time even if somebody is late. Stick to the time frame and stop somebody if he uses too much time. Meetings have to be effective and short.

- Mistake 1 – The person who hires does not know the job himself and work which needs to be done. The direct manager of a future employee must be in the interview and accept his new subordinate. If he does not want him, don't hire.

- Mistake 2 - Presentation skills of the candidate are valued more than his performance. Even the best candidate can be nervous at the interview.

- Mistake 3 – Don't try to change people. It is not worth. Focus on what they already have in them and build on it. Don't focus on removing their weaknesses, focus on building on their strengths.

A very good book on management is *John Adair's Handbook of Management and Leadership*. You will find here that managing other people starts with managing yourself and I consider this book with its techniques the basic study material for managers. I highly recommend that you read it.

Example of operation manual for sales manager (SM)
Responsibilities

SM is responsible for achieving sales plan, which is confirmed by his manager at the end of each year. Plan consists of monthly income, monthly costs and monthly cash flow. If achieved at 80% and more of the cash flow plan, SM will get 2% of net income as a bonus.

SM is responsible to act in compliance with company's values and mission.

Profile

SM is disciplined, reliable, self-reliant, systematic person with analytical thinking who learns quickly. SM cares about details, is customer and profit oriented.

Importance of employee's position

SM is a key employee as he increases positive cash flow, which is necessary for covering all company's expenditures. If his performance does not meet expected criteria, every employee will get smaller reward.

Manual

Rules: All advertising done by SM have to be under 20% CPO. Expected average is 15% CPO.

...etc.

This is just shortened example of what manual could look like. Manuals are more specific, but it is good to keep them as short as possible. Ideal length is one page, so that the employee can read it more often. It is good to give employee short memo with 1-7 most important goals for his position. He should read it every morning and it should remind him why his work is important and what results you expect him to reach.

Purpose and persistence

Even the best people working for you (including you) need to be reminded from time to time about the basic rules of your company's system. People do forget and do lose focus. It is caused by repetitious daily activities or by unplanned emergencies, where the rules are bent a little. They need to be reminded about their purpose regularly. Check to see if they know their purpose. It may sound silly, but it is better to be silly and encourage a good job instead of being cool and encouraging a bad job. You have to remind your people **why** their work is important and **why** is the mission of the company important. Otherwise they will forget. It is natural, as we focus on day-to-day operations solving today's problems and we keep forgetting the big picture if not reminded. You can give your people written memos to remind them, but expect that some will not read them. They consider it waste of time, because "they know it already".

Doing a task must make sense to people; otherwise they will start putting it down the priority list and then erase it completely from to do list. People seek purpose of their work and you as a manager have to give it to them. Living a life without a purpose is not a life of happiness. The same goes for work – working and not being identified with the work's purpose does not add to person's happiness. With the work's purpose in your heart, you will feel satisfied when the work is done. If you feel empty after finishing the work, you may not understand the work's purpose or you are not identified with it. Maybe it is not the right work for you.

What most people miss is to have their place in a community that has a purpose, an order, and a meaning. Your company can be that community.

Enthusiasm

Use the power of enthusiasm. It is catchy and it forces people to react. If leaders are not enthusiastic about their goals, they can't expect their followers to be fiery for their goals. Enthusiasm needs desire and conviction.

You can light enthusiasm in yourself by doing your work like you love it and by fully concentrating on your work. By pretending it, it will become your habit to love your work and fully concentrate on it. Your enthusiasm will be very visible and even without any words you will shine it on your followers. If they see how happy you are when you work, they will try to copy your behavior. When you will feel enthusiasm, your worries, tiredness, and stress will diminish.

Charismatic people are enthusiastic. They are interested in goals of other people and seek the good characteristics in others, and they work on their own personal improvement and give praise. People will judge you by 1. What you do. 2. How you look. 3. What you say. 4. How you say it.

Advices on leadership

- If two or more people decide on their goal and they dedicate their life to the goal, there is nothing they can't reach. You as a leader are the bearer of that goal and you have to keep it in mind all the time.
- As a leader you have to use the talent and time of other people. You have to show them the better future you are going towards.
- Lead only people who deserve it. Don't lead everybody who needs it. Some people are too lazy to be beneficial for the community or they simply are not made to be lead. If they don't obey the rules you have in your community, get rid of them before they infect others. Don't waste your time and energy with them. You are a better leader if you use that energy on people who deserve it.
- The best leaders have a strong will and are humble. Being humble does not mean being weak. It means to have your ego under control and recognize there is something bigger than you.
- Leaders are public speakers. Some people are afraid of public speaking. The best way to conquer fear of public speaking is to … speak in public. It is that simple. There is no secret to it. All you have to do is to prepare for your speech and then do it as often as you can. You will get used to it and then you will have no problem speaking in public. You have to believe in what you say and your speech must be believable. Work on your body language and emotions as well. Stating the facts is not enough; people have to believe you on an emotional level. Emotions always win over

rational mind. If you are afraid of your bad speech, focus on the people you speak to. If you are focused on how you want to help those people by delivering them critical information, you will have no time to think about mistakes you make. You are there to help them, and if you help them, they will remember that help, not how many mistakes you made. Speak naturally just like you speak with your friends. Your audience is combined of regular people. They are not much different from you or me. Even if they are presidents of large companies or countries, they are just people. They also have to eat like you, they also have to sleep like you, and they also have to visit the restroom just like you do. Yes, and they also make mistakes just like you do.

- The road to greatness is not by having a lot of people serve you. The road to greatness is by finding out the best way for you to serve others. First you have to help them and then you will get what you want in exchange.
- If you promise something, fulfill it. Break your promise only if you want to get rid of the person.
- Integrity – be yourself; don't pretend to be someone else. Your words and actions need to be in harmony.
- Act based only on verified information, not based on gossip.
- Make sure you understand what others say. Listening to and understanding is not the same. Use your ears, eyes, and also your heart. Summarize what you heard to confirm you got it right.
- Take interest also in your people, not just in

their performance. Understand their motives.
- Express your ideas, plans, and emotions to your subordinates.
- If you catch someone doing something right, praise him. Don't take credit for other people's work. Give credit to those who really did it. Praise every success, even a small one. Praise must be objective and specific to be distinguished from the flattery. Praise is done with good intention; flattery is a manipulative technique to gain something from the person in exchange.
- Stand behind your people if they get into problems and offer them your helping hand.
- For others to respect your ideas, you have to respect the ideas of others.
- Never tell someone "You are wrong", if possible. If he is wrong and you have some time, give him questions, which will lead him to the correct answer. Let him save his face.
- Let others speak. If you listen, you will understand more than if you speak.
- If you want someone to accept your idea, persuade him that it was his idea, not yours.
- Lead others with questions, not with answers.
- There is no shame in a detailed analysis of what went wrong. You have to do it to understand what caused the problem. You have to focus on problem solving and not on putting the blame on people who could prevent the problem.
- Don't judge the person. Rather, judge the actions of that person and the problem. You can judge the ideas of a person, but don't judge his intelligence. Never criticize the person, just his actions.

- Solve just one problem at a time. This means you have to react quickly if the problem is found. Don't wait for monthly performance dialogue. If you try to postpone the errors the person made and then you try to solve them all at once, the person will feel attacked.
- Explain your point of view and show benefits of your solution.
- Expect yourself to grow as a person and you will soon fill your expectations. Do the same with others – Expect them to be better and they will become better.
- If you deal with people, expect you are dealing with emotional beings. Don't expect them to behave logically.
- Let your people find solutions to the problems by themselves.
- If your employee is not doing something right, begin by telling him how you are happy about some other activity, where his performance is very good. Then tell him why it is important to properly do the wrong activity. Allow him to determine and tell you his solution that will prevent him from doing the activity wrong again.
- If you are the one who is being criticized, stay calm, breathe, and listen to the person. Let your partner finish. Don't assume what he is going to tell you. People are emotional beings, filter every criticism that is irrational, and throw it away before it can do damage. Make sure you understand the rational criticism and repeat it with other words. If you think the critic is right, be prepared to change your behavior. He is criticizing your behavior, not yourself, even if he chose wrong words to express it. Keep to just

the facts and thank him for his feedback. It is O.K. to take your time to think about what was said if you need to calm yourself down. Agree on future steps to prevent your negative behavior.
- Before you say you don't agree with someone, make sure that you really don't agree with him. Often it is just problem of misunderstanding.

How to praise

When you praise, you encourage repetitive action or behavior. You have to be specific to encourage what you want. Otherwise a person who is praised can understand your words in a different way and will do something else next time.

1. **Be specific**. Instead of saying "*Good job*" Say "Good job explaining benefits of our strategy to our stakeholders with such enthusiasm."
2. **Praise often**, even two or three times a day. Yes, you can praise the same behavior multiple times to remind the praised person what he did right.
3. **Praise as soon as possible** after positive action.
4. Never use criticism in the same sentence as praising. Many people connect praise with criticism by using the "but" word. This negates the praise. Use separate sentences for praise and criticism.

Business plan

When you plan your business, you have to know how the business will look when it is finished. Many people plan to sell their business and this can be their ultimate goal – when they sell it, it is finished.

From business plan to successful sale of the company, there is very long and hard road. The road is not for quitters as there will be lots of problems that you need to solve. Business is mostly about solving someone else's problems and being paid for it. If you solve big problems, your reward can be big.

1. You have to give your company a purpose. What will it do?
2. Values of the company employees – who we are and how we behave. If you are a single person start up, you can skip this step for now.
3. Customers – who are our customers, why they purchase from us and how we will communicate with them. What problems do we solve for them?
4. List of important activities and property which are necessary for successful running of the business. To each activity or property add a few words how will you get and keep it.
5. Who will we cooperate with? Who will do the accounting, which lawyer will we contact if we will have legal questions, and who else will help us?
6. Schedule of activities to be done. What needs to be done first? Where do we want to get in 10 years, 5 years, 3 years, next year? What steps are necessary to do today, next week, next month?
7. Cash flow plan and a budget plan.

A business plan can be just one page long. The simpler it gets the better for the beginning. It is good to simplify. The plan has to answer just 4 questions:

1. Where we are now?

2. Where do we want to get?
3. How will we get there?
4. Who will help us to get there?

Often for the investors, the last question is the most important. They prefer the second best plan with the best management. It is because plans will be changed when they crash with the reality. Good management will know how to adjust the plan to reach its goals.

There are a few more questions that should be answered, but the critical ones are these four. Investors are interested in questions like: Is your business able to grow and use economy of scale? Does your business have unique selling propositions? Was the idea behind your business already tested by the market? Whose problem does your business solve? Are your plans and numbers realistic?

Six tips that will get you started

1. When you get a good idea about how to create assets, act fast. One good idea and disciplined action is all you need to become wealthy. Most people will fail to act because they are afraid of failing, so you will have clear advantage over majority of people. Use that advantage and don't waste your time.

2. Start moving and stay in motion. Inertia will help you. It is much easier to keep and increase inertia than to start and stop multiple times. Starting is the most difficult part. Do something that brings you closer to your goal every day. Make yourself doomed to succeed. Warriors in the past sometimes burned their ships to limit their options. With burned ships at their backs, their only option was to assault their enemies in front of them and succeed because they had nothing to lose. If you limit your options to one choice, your focus and chance to succeed will increase dramatically.

3. Fast tempo is what you need for success. You will get more accomplished and you will not miss many opportunities. Do more in less time.

4. Review your tasks constantly. Search for options on how to get it done with minimum time and effort.

5. When you fear something, get rid of your fear by fully focusing on your goal. You can accomplish anything you decide to accomplish. Find someone who already did what you want to do. If he could do it, you can do it. When you fear something, take that fear and analyze it.

The more you know about it, the less you will fear. Do what you fear to do and your fear will get weaker.

6. The first step of business is the courage to start realizing your business plan. The second step is to keep going on. Perseverance is important. Every single time you keep going on regardless of obstacles, your make your self-discipline stronger and you build up your character.

Real estate owner

Real estate is assets used for long-term passive income (generated through renting the property) and to protect your money from inflation (as a capital gain). If your costs including tax are higher than your income, it is not an asset, but a liability. If the market crashes and prices of houses go down, your capital gain will be negative. Yes, there are risks also in real estate.

Rich people do invest in real estate and that is the reason you have to know more about it. Good real estate property and precious metals like gold and silver are the usual way to secure your wealth. Precious metals may keep value, but they do not make cash flow until you sell them. Good real estate brings you rental cash and keeps or grows in value. The price of precious metals and real estate fluctuates and this means that after you purchase them, their price can go down or up. That's why you should buy them only when they generate positive cash flow or if their price is lower compared to their long-term average.

As you probably already know, the most important thing when choosing the right property is the location of the real estate. Location, location, location is the main reason for your real estate to be rented or vacant. Once you purchased it, there are many modifications you can make to increase the value of your property, but you can't change its location.

The price of real estate you purchase must be profitable according to your calculations. Have limits for location and square feet available. Never buy property if your calculations don't show you it will be profitable and it will generate positive cash flow. You can find average rent prices of analyzed location in Internet advertisements offering rental property. Then you calculate all the costs and deduct the costs from the average rental price to see if your cash flow will be positive. Don't forget to implement taxes into your calculation. Many small landlords accept only cash payments to avoid the taxes.

Look around the property. Are there shops, hospitals, schools, parks? Is the environment safe and clean? What kinds of neighbors live there? What is the state of buildings around? Are they well maintained? Are people leaving the area or are they moving in? Is there hidden opportunity to increase rental income?

One type of hidden opportunity can be restructuring one big apartment into two smaller ones, which will generate higher cash flow. That's, of course, an opportunity only if tenants in that area are looking for small apartments and there is not enough of them.

Real estate property is expensive. Never rush into buying and having no option to cancel the contract. Give yourself a few days to think it through and have somebody more experienced to advise you. It can be a friend who already purchased apartments in that area and has made mistakes himself. This way you can avoid his mistakes and make a better deal. Don't feel bad when you look very closely to the walls and ceilings for signs of mold or cracks as you can negotiate a lower price, because of the defects and you will have to pay for reconstruction later.

If you can't find a profitable apartment, don't buy the best one you can find but wait. You can wait even a year until you find the right property, but that is

O.K. If the property does not look profitable, why should you buy it? I read that Donald Trump waited 20 years to finish his real estate property deal. If he could wait, you can wait too.

Once your calculations show it is profitable, ask your advisor to look at it and if he thinks the numbers will work, negotiate the deal. Most sellers publish higher prices than what they are really willing to sell it for. It is O.K. to bid 10-30% less than their initial asking price. If they are desperate to sell, they will sell with a huge discount. Real estate is a popular way to get rich, because you can spend 0 to 30% of your money on a down payment and borrow the rest of the money from the bank, purchasing the property and enjoying positive cash flow from the rental property until the price of the property rises in few years. Then you can flip it for other property with huge profit.

A secret of a successful real estate owner is to find great deals. Great deals are those that you can buy cheap, increase the value of the property with good management, and keep the property for positive cash flow until you sell the property with huge profit. You never know if the market price of the property will rise or drop, so you have to invest both for capital gain and positive cash flow. If the price drops, you still have positive cash flow and you can keep the property as long as you need. If the location is right and property is well maintained, sooner or later the price will go up just because of the inflation. If the property is not profitable and you can't keep positive cash flow from it during the bad times, you made a purchasing mistake with the property. Profit is made when you are purchasing the asset.

Real estate investing check list

Answer the following questions before you sign a real estate deal:

- Who will be the tenant and how much will you receive as rental cash? What is the average rental price for similar property in the area?

- Why should you pay such high interest for the mortgage? Push the bankers for as lower interest rate as possible.

- How much will you get in positive cash flow from the property per month?

- What is the ROI value you expect from the property?

- Does this property fit your long term investing strategy? When you will have to exit the property and what is your exit strategy?

- What vacancy rate do you expect?

- How much will you pay for maintenance, electricity, water, gas, repairs, various fees and taxes?

- What are the plans for the area? Are there any noisy constructions to be expected? Will the companies in the area hire or lay off people? Is the population growing or dropping in the area?

- What drives the trend of real estate price in the area and for how long do you expect the trend to go this way?

- How long can you support your investment if it

will stay vacant and what is the breaking point of exiting from the investment?

Your first R/E investing can be based on following steps:

1. Analyze 100 properties to see if they look profitable based on sales price, average rental price, and costs. The first data you need to know is how much will you get in rental price each month. This is the basic value for your calculations before you negotiate the price with the seller and the monthly mortgage costs with the bank.

2. Secure financing of the property with the bank.

3. Take a look at the 10 best properties if they are looking profitable and make the sellers an offer. The offer has to be indefinite and you have to be able to cancel the offer without any obligations.

4. Get 3 properties approved by the owner and by your bank. Check again based on new data if the property will generate positive cash flow each month.

5. Buy one property and rent it.

6. Manage your first properties to get knowledge and experience about R/E management.

Rules for managing R/E property

- Prepare rules and guide line for advertising the property.

- Filter your tenants thoroughly – they have to meet certain criteria. It can be criteria like not having committed a crime, good enough income, credit check for late payments in the past, and calling last two R/E managers where they lived before to see if there were any troubles with the tenant.

- The contract – check contracts of other local R/E managers. The contract must contain data about dates of payments, penalties for late payments, maximum people allowed to live in the property, rules for removing the tenant, what repairs and costs will be done and paid by the tenant and what by the landlord, procedures if neighbors will complain about the tenant, height of annual rental price growth, rules for pets living in the property, and warranty deposit.

- Start with small investments and get experience in buying, managing and selling the properties. Look for R/E in your area to keep easier control over them.

- Create your real estate investment due diligence checklist.

- A contract for purchasing property must give you the right to cancel if you find out something you were not told about the property (seller does not have to lie to you, sometimes he simple do not know about certain flaws of the property). You are purchasing the property and you take huge risks, so contract has to protect you from those risks. E.g., you can pay last 30% of price after a month spent living in that property to make sure there are no hidden flaws.

- In optimal circumstances the day you buy the property it will be rented to tenant.

- Become a member of landlord association or get to know other landlords and get experience from them.

Paper assets owner

You have to understand that money markets and capital markets can be manipulated by big players and also that the market does not behave rationally as we were taught at schools. Even if fundamental data tells us that when the central bank is printing money not covered by any production, the price of solid commodities like gold should rise. I have experienced the opposite – it was manipulated by announcing selling of multiple tons of gold. In reality it is hard to say if the gold which was sold as a paper bill was not sold multiple times, because that is what banks do – with partial reserves they can sell the same money or the same gold they have multiple times. They are selling something they do not have on a regular basis.

Don't try to become rich too quickly when you invest your money. The only thing you can get quickly with the money invested is losing it quickly. Investing must be preceded by investigating. Looking for great deals in which you will invest should take as much time as you spent earning that money. If you, for example, want to invest and trade on the Foreign Exchange 10,000 dollars and you spent one year putting that money into your investment account, you should spend one year on learning how to trade on Forex. Consider playing on a demo account for one year and after you get sustainable and profitable results, only then invest your real money.

A good investment adviser also invests in the products he sells and he is constantly educating himself in area of his business. A good broker is the one who creates profit for you and the bad one is the one who creates excuses for you.

When looking for a good broker, ask for their best in your investment amount range. If they can't give you one or two names and say all are very good, go to another company. Ask the broker to show you their best investment opportunities and why he thinks they are the best. Find out what his evaluation criteria are and if they are the same criteria as yours. If your broker makes you rich, reward him above average, so that he will call you first when he finds another great deal. Use advisers who are smarter and better informed than you. In a best case scenario, your adviser also invests his money into assets he offers to you.

The easiest thing you can do with your money is to lose it. Even if your adviser looks like he is responsible and trustworthy, but your gut tells you otherwise (you don't know why but you simply do not trust him), don't do business with him. The best sign people want to use you is that they try to put you under pressure and persuade you that this is once in a lifetime opportunity. They usually talk too much about how you can trust them. When the investment looks too good to be true, it usually is. Learn from my mistake with Jozef. I wrote about it earlier in this book.

First thing you should have in mind when dealing with an adviser is that you take full responsibility for your life and your decisions. An adviser does what his name says – he gives you advice. The decision, what to do with that advice, is fully up to you. Take advice from your advisers, think about their opinions and facts they supply you with, and then make a decision.

Intellectual property owner

Intellectual property (IP) is a legal concept that refers to creations of the mind for which exclusive rights are recognized. The stated objective of most intellectual property law (with the exception of trademarks) is to "Promote progress." By exchanging limited exclusive rights for disclosure of inventions and creative works, society and the patent/copyright owner mutually benefit, and an incentive is created for inventors and authors to create and disclose their work. Some commentators have noted that the objective of intellectual property legislators and those who support its implementation appears to be "absolute protection." The idea is that the creators will not have sufficient incentive to invent unless they are legally entitled to capture the full social value of their inventions.

When we speak about IP, it does not have to be just trademarks or patents. It can be a person as well. Look at famous sportsmen, singers or actors – they are their own brand. Their name, face, and what they say has value for others and companies are willing to pay them to promote their products. Many sportsmen, singers and actors usually get richer by promoting products than by their regular performance income.

Creating a brand around your person is a very difficult and time consuming task. I recommend you to search YouTube for Will Smith interview where he shares his wisdom on how to get famous and rich. Determination, sacrifice, and hard work worked well for him and it will work well for you if you chose to follow this path.

Protection of IP is an important subject for its

owner. IP and mostly trademarks, know-how, and patents are very important subjects also in business. If you can't legally protect your property, others will use it as they wish. Different countries have different laws for IP and even if your competitor breaks the law in your country, it does not mean that he broke any law in his country. IP protection must be your subject of study if you want to become intellectual property owner. Good book I read on IP is from <u>Michael A. Lechter – Protecting Your #1 Asset</u>.

Where can you learn and get experience

Study books, read articles

By studying books and articles you can learn the basics of your knowledge. With theory in your head you will be able to better understand what is going on in real world and why things happen.

All leaders are readers. You should read books to improve quality of your life. Look for How-to do books as they contain practical tips for improvement. If you do want to save time, you can listen to audio books while driving or while doing something else. What is important is to skip books of insignificant value. Don't waste your time. Before you start reading a book, go through the reviews and table of contents to find out if it is worth to read the book. In last chapter I have put together a list of the best books I ever read in the end of this book to help you at the beginning. Take notes of important ideas you read in a book, it will later save your time. Keep a journal.

Mentor/coach

Choose a mentor in areas you want to improve. It has to be person who already successfully has done what you want to do. Find as much as you can about what that person did and how he or she did it. Read their biographies and learn from their experience.

If that person is available for you to contact, prepare list of questions and contact him or her. Offer them something small, such as lunch, for their time and ask them what to do and also what not to do. Take notes of their advice as they are priceless. If you can't meet face to face, call them or write them an e-mail. Try to step out of the crowd in an appropriate way as they may have hundreds of e-mails per month similar to yours. If you face a problem, ask your mentor. If he is not available, ask yourself what your mentor would do.

Seminars/classes

When you will be attending seminars, choose the ones that also have workshops. You don't have to attend a seminar just to listen to the lecturer and leave with notes of what he said. Usually you can buy good book on that subject and you will get it cheaper and save your hand while writing the notes.

What you can get on a seminar: 1. Experience in doing what you are learning (usually under supervision of the lecturer), 2. Answers to your questions from the lecturer (if it is part of the agenda), 3. Contacts and answers from fellow students.

When you decide to attend a seminar, have questions ready based on knowledge you already got from reading books and practicing yourself. Be prepared, because good seminars are costly. Use your time spent at the seminar wisely by being prepared. Sit in the front row to get as much information as possible. You can search for classes that are free or for a very low fee. You can try also free government subsidiary classes. Search and you will find.

Always ask yourself what is the goal of the lecturer. Does he profit from teaching or does he profit from selling you his other services after the seminar? Is he really giving you advice that will make you rich, or is he giving you advice that will make him rich? The goal of a broker is not to make you rich, but to make you do as many purchase/sell transactions as possible, because he is paid a commission from every transaction. Even when he is paid a percentage from profit he earns you, he can decide to focus on short-term gain from transaction fees, as my broker did to me.

Instead of 50% of all profits he would earn from my investments controlled by him, he decided to "clean" my account and earn on transaction fees, so I found out that he made too many transactions to keep it profitable. I repeat the story, because it is a very important lesson for you. This was the way that I quickly lost money, so be careful. You will be cheated from time to time by liars – what you can do is to observe people really well and decide if they can be trusted. Liars have a common characteristic way of talking and doing things. Be cautious when a person tells you very often "you can trust me", etc. Trustworthy people consider their word unbreakable liability, so they do not speak about it that much. People who break promises usually speak about trustworthiness, trustworthy people don't.

When you see those characteristics, you will know that he or she is probably a liar. Liars will lie to you if it suits him, you can bet on it. Why? Because he is a liar – he does not see lying as something bad. You can bet on the fact that he will lie to get an advantage. You have to spend time with a person to know if he is a liar or not. Try it with your friends or colleagues – if you are a trustworthy person, they can tell you their secrets and you will understand them more. If they speak about cheating their mate (they will of course tell you also why it is their mate's fault and not theirs) you can bet that this person will cheat also you if it suits him. What he does is normal to him and the worst feelings he can have is that you were stupid enough not to expect he will lie to you. So or so, it will be always your fault to a liar – either you were stupid enough not to see his lie or you are not tolerant enough to understand why he "had to" do it. Do NOT expect him to regret his lies. It is NEVER their fault in their mind. If they consider it fault at all.

The more you interact with people, the more experience you will get with finding out who can be trusted and who cannot. When you find out you are dealing with a liar, you will have to decide if you still want to do business with him. Sometimes you will not be able to find an "honorable man" when you will need a partner to do business quickly. You will have to decide if you cancel the business or accept that your partner will lie to you and be ready for it.

Learning by becoming an employee

The safest way to learn necessary skills is by being an employee in a company, which will pay for your training and for your time. This is great because you will not only learn what you need to by doing it and getting experience, but you will also earn money for a living. With seminars you have to pay for them, but with hardworking employee status, you will get money for learning and practicing, while someone else will pay for your training.

By visiting college you can get academic education and lots of contacts you can use in the future. By working you can get money, professional education, contacts and experience. What is better for you? Job or school? It is great that if you are hard worker with lot of energy and you are willing to exchange your free time for your career, you can find good job where you will earn for your living, get professional education and build social links with people you work with, you can study during weekends to get academic education and more social contacts which you can use in the future.

During your free time, when you are not exercising your body to keep it healthy, you can start your own business project. You can even earn money by studentship. I have done this and let me tell you, this is very energy and time consuming. You will probably have no time for your friends and hobbies. It took me 3 years to burn out. Luckily I had finished my PhD. by that time, started our first company, and quit my job. It was hard, but with two incomes, it helped me to build some capital. Having that capital enabled me to be on the investing part of starting company. If I would not have two incomes, I would not be able to accumulate that capital easily. If you are afraid to start your own business, start with a job and an academic education with scholarship.

In your own business

Starting and running your own business can be a freeing activity that will give you huge financial rewards if successful. If you see the statistics, 50% of new businesses will fail within first five years. Some sources state that 80% of new business will fail within first five years. Various sources state various data, but the point is clear – you have a better chance of quitting your company within the first five years than to keep operating it. It is a hard job to start and run a business. Be prepared for big problems, but never give up.

However, the experience you will get in your own business is priceless. You will learn a lot at your successes and even more on your mistakes. You will learn a lot about yourself. Expect problems and expect yourself to solve them. With each problem solved you will grow as a person. Your goal should be to create money machine serving people and your personal growth. What you will become is more important than what you get from the business.

It is wise to protect yourself in your business by running your company with limited liability and paying yourself first. I was paying everyone else first during my first year of business and kept just what was left. It was not much. I paid three times more in taxes then what I earned for myself. Have clearly written down rules for your business on how it will pay you, when will the company be finished, and when you will let it go.

By investing experience

It is safer first to get a book with tips how to invest than to start investing immediately. Diversify information you find into facts and opinions of the author. Some advice you will read is bullshit. Filter them and keep just what suits your strategy and personality. Take your time learning before you invest. Be aware of those websites or people who are offering you "help" with investing your money. Don't give them control of your money. You must keep the control of your money for yourself. The worst that you can do is to tell people around you that you have some spare money you would like to invest and you do not know where to put it. Financial piranhas will gather around you and will offer you their service. Remember that they can promise you anything you want to hear, but most important is what they can guarantee and if you will be able to make them fulfill their part of the contract.

When you have studied investing for some time and you feel confident that you will be able to invest with profits, take baby steps and invest only money you are willing to lose in the process, because there is a high probability, that your first investments will be a loss. It is what statistics tell us. Most people fail with their investments. Your loss is someone else's profit. Take the loss as the price for your training and experience.

Six steps that will make you successful

Write down what do you want to get from your life. This can take some time and lot of rewriting. Reevaluate your goal once or twice a year to make sure if it is still what you really want. What you want changes over time as you better understand yourself and as your initial goals are completed. It may not look easy, but once you split your year goals into monthly and weekly goals, they do not seem impossible to reach. Do not limit yourself in your dreams and do not write down the dreams of someone else. Don't write down dreams of your parents or friends. Write down what you want.

I started to record my financial plans in 2008 and my personal development plans in 2009 after realizing that who I am is more important than what I have. My focus over the years shifted from money and academic study to self-defense/survival study and then back again to money after I stopped being afraid of my physical elimination.

You will have to adapt your plans according to the situation and priorities in your life. Don't worry if you make mistakes in your plans. You will learn also from your mistakes if you pay attention. Because a big loss hurts so much, it will burn the lesson learned into your mind and your body.

Most personal plans include family, relationships, financial, physical and spiritual health. There should be items like how much money will you earn, spend and keep, what subjects will you study and practice, what skills will you get, and who of your friends will you knowingly spend your time with.

For most people areas like relationships, work, money, and health are a good starting place in search of a happier life. Write down what goals you want to reach in those areas and think about what kind of person you have to be to reach your goals. Later as you will understand yourself more deeply, you will skip items that you would like to have, but you don't want them so badly that you are willing to sacrifice other items.

Now write down what you want and when you want it.

I want	Date

1. Do you really, really want it?

There is a big difference between items you consider nice to have and those which you really want. You want them so much that you will not mind sacrificing all those nice to have items. Believe your dream is possible to achieve and decide if you are willing to pay the price needed to reach it. If you have doubts, look for people who have already done what you want to do. If they did it, you can do it too. Don't tell me they had it easier, you were not walking in their shoes, so you can't tell they had it easier. I don't care for your excuses. All you need to know is they managed to do it and that is why it is also possible to do it for you. If you really want it, you will find a way to reach your goal.

Most self-made rich people had it difficult in childhood and solving problems made them stronger. If conditions in your country do not allow you to reach a really high goal, find a way to move to a country where it is possible. Today's world is global. Don't limit yourself to one country. If you really want to achieve high goals, you have to risk, study, and work hard on yourself. The harder you are, the easier it is to reach your goals. If you can dream of something, you can achieve it. Visualize it – keep your eyes and mind on your goal each morning – it will help you to decide what is important and what is not. Focus on your purpose in life – that is what is important – to fulfill your life's purpose. Once you find your life's purpose and you work on it every day - that is what will make you happy. It will make you happy not just for a moment, but for the rest of your life.

Remember – the harder it is, the stronger you will become. Imagine for a moment that you already reached your goal. How does it feel? Take few minutes and let the feelings of your success flow through your body and your soul. You are good enough to get whatever you want, don't limit yourself to today's reality.

Don't cheat, take those few minutes and let the

feelings of success make you happy. How you felt?

Was your soul happy with this image? Is it what you really want? Is it your purpose in life? Look inside you and to your feelings. Most people, when they think of their **real** life purpose, feel willies in their neck and spine. Listen to your body and your soul. Your soul can speak to you just through your feelings. Those feelings don't have to be only pleasant. Your purpose can be to prevent something and then you can be motivated also by anger, fear and compassion. Your soul can speak to you through your tears.

You can have multiple purposes in your life. Most common purpose is to survive and to take care of your children and your family. These are the basic purposes. There are also your higher purposes. If you don't know what your higher purpose is – study, watch and try new things and take notes of how you felt. The stronger emotions you get, the closer you are to your higher purpose.

2. Goals setting

When you have written down what dream you really want to reach, it is good idea to write it down as a goal. Goals must be measurable and specific. For setting goals there is a technique called SMART. You should re-write your goal until it is Specific, Measurable, Attainable, Relevant, Timely.

Specify exactly what you want. Otherwise you can get something slightly different than what you imagined. For example, if you write down you want to own an apartment. If you won't make it specific, like – I want to own a new, comfortable and equipped 3-room 860 square foot apartment in downtown New York, you could end up having a 2-room home in Alaska.

This is why you need to **be specific**.

If your goal is, for example, to be healthy, how will you **measure** that? There are many ways and one of them is to define your goal, such as if you are healthy, you wake up full of energy, and go to bed smiling 365 days a year. And you can keep track of your health during the years. You may find it interesting if you find out that you are getting ill, for example, each February, or when the temperature drops to 14 degrees Fahrenheit.

A goal is **attainable** when you or your team has the abilities and resources to reach it. A **relevant** goal is worthwhile for you to work on right now. A **timely** goal has a deadline and, usually for bigger goals, it has deadlines for partial goals as well.

After you are satisfied with your written down goals, make a list of everything that you will have to do to achieve this goal and put a deadline to each of those smaller actions. If you don't know what needs to be done, study the subject first. Go from the final goal to the present day and arrange activities in sequence so you will know what has to be done before something else can be done. For each action, set a priority. Now you have a plan. Start with critical actions that influence your goal the most. Leave low priority activities for later. Critical activities are the one to start with, because ... because they are critical to achieve your goal of course. You can work yourself to death spending time on low priority activities and not get closer to your goal. Always start with the most important task.

You should now have quite a clear picture of what needs to be done. Most of time plans have to be adapted as there will be activities where you depend on other people and some of them will not keep agreed deadline. Or you will become ill and your plan will be postponed. This happens all the time. IT systems go down, people get ill, they forget they had something to do for you or they put it on their low priority list, etc.

You should have a clear picture now of what needs to be done to reach your goals. When you see the tasks, ask yourself again if the final goal is worth all the trouble.

Create visualization of your optimal future if everything goes good for 5 years. What does your optimal future look like? Write it down and use pictures.

Now sit down and write what you desire from your life and make short plan how will you get it. A few sentences are enough.

3. Action plan

Believe in yourself and start today! You can achieve anything you can imagine. I really mean anything. If my goal was to change the way people travel, I could start developing a company that will (probably with government military funds) create teleports like we saw in Star Trek movies. If it will not be achieved in my lifetime, the company I created will invent teleportation after my death, but it will be done. Don't listen to anyone tell you it can't be done. Anything can be done. I will give you an example of a one-year plan.

My 2011 plan:

1. I want a monthly income of 2000 €, expenses 800 €, and keep 1200 € for investing. *Although I have not met that income each month I have overachieved it in other months and my year income plan was fulfilled to 221%. Also my expenses were higher than planed and I fulfilled my expenses plan to 131% as I got some unexpected costs. My plan for money to keep was fulfilled to 281% and I was satisfied. In 2011, I was focused mostly on income generation.*
2. I want to practice Systema a lot to be able to defend myself and my family on the street.
3. I want to keep athletic and healthy body.
4. I want to master the whole process of starting and running a business including finding employees, managing, evaluating, rewarding and firing them. This goal included understanding legal, tax, accounting, financial, marketing and, most importantly, the sales part of running a business.
5. I want to master negotiations and deal making.
6. I want to have equipment and skills for long-term survival in forest.

Good. Now you know what you want and when you want it. Divide your goals into partial goals that can be reached within one year. Finished? Now you have your first year plan. Start with a maximum of 6 tasks, which have biggest influence on your results and put the rest to later dates. Starting with the most important tasks will probably be harder as you will be afraid of making mistakes with them. You will probably want to start with minor tasks to warm up, right? Well, those minor tasks can take all your time and energy and you can end up without even starting the important ones. You have to start with tasks that have biggest influence on reaching your goals. You can think about it, but it has to be done this way. If you don't believe me, try both approaches and see which has better results.

O.K. Now put the most important tasks into your first month plan and the rest into the remaining eleven months. A few sentences for each month are enough to give you a general direction for writing weekly and daily plans for that particular month. Your plans should be written in positive results of your activity. This will help you to avoid working for the sake of working, instead working to get results as fast as possible. If you get your results faster than planned, reward yourself. I used to reward myself with starting activities that were planned for the following month. It resulted in my frustration, because when I pressed two month activities into one month and I did not get the results for both months, I started to blame myself for lack of results. When you finish your monthly tasks, celebrate first, remind yourself how clever you are, and only then start with additional tasks. Give yourself feedback of success first.

The same goes for the weekly plans. At the beginning of a new month I put deadlines of monthly activities into week plans. My week plan consists of quite specific day plans. Don't forget to give yourself time to relax at least one day a week in your plans. When your day plan is read in the morning, put the items in order according to their priority and begin with the most important tasks first. I added pictures of what I want to accomplish that year to my week plan, so I keep focus on my year goals. Visualization is very important as our brain operates in pictures.

Monthly plan example:

May	Parachute jump - learn the theory and practice. Write short eBook on online selling.
June	Purchase garden for my father - price 3000 €. Get financing for 3-room apartment with 100% financing if possible, get mortgage offer directly from bank and then ask "independent" mortgage consultant for his terms if he can offer better terms. Learn to drive race karts. Cliff jumping 10 times to conquer my fear.
July	Learn to drive motorbike and lorry. Research for government orders on unemployed people training to improve their qualification. Research on Inside contacts in government bureaus for their purchase needs.

In the beginning of the month I divide monthly goals to smaller tasks and give them a deadline. Example: 8th May – find companies selling parachute jump and chose one according to price, reputation, and distance. Then contact Peter and invite him to go with you. 10th May – purchase coupon for parachute jump and note the date. Then I create tasks for the week before jumping – study parachute jumping theory to get most of the training. Next task – write short eBook on online selling would be like – 1st May – put your notes on online selling together. Remove duplicates. Create table of contents for the eBook. 2nd May – read how-to articles on eBook creation and adjust the table of contents. 31st May – finish the eBook. 5th May – finish first chapter. 12th May – finish second chapter. 19th May – finish third chapter. 26th May – finish fourth chapter. Then I sort all partial task of the month according to their date and copy them to weekly plan.

Week plan example:

	Start	Finish	Break	Work
Mon				0
Tue	8:30	17:30	1:00	8
Wed	8:30	20:30	2:00	10
Thu	9:30	16:30	2:00	5
Fri	12:30	21:30	1:00	8
Sat	8:30	18:30	1:00	9
Sun	10:30	22:30	3:00	9
Sum				49

25	Mon	Prepare weekly plan. Reading education articles and videos.
26	Tue	Write book. Meet Rado.
27	Wed	Write book. Sauna.
28	Thu	Send sales letter. Write book. Salsa lessons.
29	Fri	Write book. Meet friends outside.
30	Sat	Write book. Household tasks. Fitness and boxing exercise. Meet friends in the evening.
31	Sun	Write book. Spend few hours in the nature. Relax.

4. Disciplined action

Discipline is probably the most important trait, which will help you on your way to success. Most people know what they should do to be successful, as the success principles are not secret. But most people are too lazy or afraid to do what needs to be done when it needs to be done. Discipline is doing activities that need to be done even if you do not feel like doing them. Only strong physical illness is adequate excuse for postponing your planned action. Postponing your actions makes your determination weaker. Take action each day. Do at least a small step to get you closer to your goal. Then make the next small step. Then put those small steps as close together as possible to build momentum of energy and success. It is like a flywheel – once it is spinning it is easy to keep it moving.

Finish one task before you start another if possible. Unfinished tasks stay in your mind, occupy your brain space. This will damage your focus and momentum. Finish your first top priority task and only then start the next one. Focus your mind completely on the task. You can't focus on three things at one time. Focus on just one task at a time. If you jump from task to task without finishing it, you are wasting time and creating stress. Avoid interruptions and this means also your colleagues.

Be disciplined and do your planned actions and measure if they are bringing you closer to your goals.

Reading books like this will not help you until you take disciplined action. Have a daily "To Do" list and also a "Stop Doing" list. They are both important. You can't do everything by yourself if you prepare something with world-class effect. Use teams to get better results. Every day in the morning do something that brings you closer to your most important goal. This will help you to keep focus.

5. Study

You become what you think about all day, so study what you want to become. Be careful with choosing what to study as it shifts your character towards what you feed your brain.

Study your subject of interest and study only quality and important sources. Do not drown yourself in data overflow or in trash information. Study how to get what you want. Know your options. Read how-to books. Don't waste your time inventing how to boil water if somebody already found that out. Time is precious, don't waste it on minor things. Learn from people who already achieved what you want to achieve. Search for practical advice, not academic advice. Search for how things work, not a theory about how they should work.

Meet successful people and talk with them about earning money and acquiring assets. Most people like to talk about their accomplishments. Spend your time with your more successful friends. I have known my friend Robo for more than 6 months and I knew he was a cool and funny guy, but I did not know how financially successful he was until I visited him in his apartment.

Don't be afraid to ask for help. If you ask for advice, your mentor will lose none of his knowledge, so don't be shy, ask for advice and use it if it suits your plans.

6. Review your plans periodically

Take time at least once a year and compare your plans to real results. Is what you are doing bringing you closer to your goal? Can you do something or stop doing something which will help you to reach your goal faster?

Review your successes just as you review your failures. Both are important. Get energy from your past successes. As you develop and learn, your goals can change. It is normal that after some time your goal is not as important to you anymore. As soon as you update what you want, update your plans and then act according to your plans.

That's it. Now get to work.

Bonus chapters

Owning vs. controlling

More important than being owner of item is to have control over the item. You should have control over things you use, like or need. For example I did not own a car until I sold my company. Being director of my company, I used the company's car. That is control. You don't have to own things to use and control them. Owning things through your company is smart because company pays taxes on difference between what it earns and what its costs are. Company spends money first and what is left gets taxed. As an individual you are taxed on everything you earn and what is left is there for you to spend. With VAT, individuals are taxed not only when they earn but also when they spend. A car is a liability; it costs money and it loses value. It is smart to control the liabilities which you need to use and let someone else pay for them.

An example of one way to lower your taxes is to buy petrol receipts for 5% of their value and use them to lower your VAT by 20% and income tax by another 19%. With this operation you could save 30.20 $ on taxes after you pay 5 $ to the person who sold you the receipts. Another benefit is that you have to take 100 $ cash from the company to level accounting costs and after you pay the petrol person 5 $, you end up with keeping 95 $ in your pocket without having to pay your personal income tax from that money. Of course I do not encourage you to do this, as this is illegal to do. But I am quite sure rich people do that all the time. All I want is to demonstrate that this can be done by business owners and to illustrate the importance of having control. From my experience, it is done very often.

100 $	Petrol receives value
5 $	Purchase of receives
20 $	VAT saving
15,20 $	Income tax saving
30,20 $	Money saved from taxation
95 $	Cash for you

Important note: Avoiding paying taxes to a good and responsible government which takes care of its citizens is wrong. But is it wrong to avoid paying taxes to government which you know is controlled by its sponsors (financial groups), who are paying for their election campaigns? Is it wrong when you know that government will use your money to pay those sponsors back instead of helping the poor or to build infrastructure cost effectively? Aren't you actually helping the criminal to prosper because you fund your corrupt government with your taxes? As a good citizen is it not your duty to keep the government and country healthy by giving it financial diet to lose all the fat which is eaten by the corrupt government sponsors? If there will be no money left to suck for those sponsors, they will leave the government employees without trying to corrupt them. And maybe not. You have to answer those questions for yourself.

I can officially encourage you only to always act

according to the laws even if the law is stupid one. Never break laws until you do control people creating the laws, people controlling the police and people controlling the judges.

You will get what you focus on and what you expect to get

All healthy people can achieve their big goal if they are dedicated to get it. Even my older sister who considers herself a loser of low confidence, low self-discipline and absence of strong will received everything she really wanted. All her goals were fulfilled in my opinion very soon. She wanted a husband, a kid, a house, a dog, to spend a lot of time with her friends and to heal kids by biofeedback. That is what she **really wanted**. Within four years she had it all. There are of course all kinds of things she **would like** to have and she will probably get them later if she decides she really wants them.

For example she would like to have her mortgage paid off, have higher salary and have a car. She is so smart that she does not have a car, but she has control over our father's car and she uses it as a taxi. Having free car with a driver is the best option of transport I could find so far. Those 'would like to have' things are not important even if she will not get them, that is why they are in the '**would like** to have' group and not in the '**really want**' group. She, like most people, would not mind if she were rich, but being rich is not on her '**I WANT**' list, it is on the 'I **would like to**' or I '**wouldn't mind to be**' list.

Everyone I know who really wanted something achieved it or is very close to achieving it soon. If a person of low confidence, low self-discipline and absence of strong will can do it, you can do it too! You just have to find out what you **really want**. After you get what you really want, focus on keeping things you really want. Focus on important things first. Keep 'would like to' lists for later.

When you study, your mind becomes focused on what you study. If you study money, your mind is focused on money and it allows you to see opportunities, which were hidden from you before. Learning means studying and obtaining experience. Don't just read what you study but take practice in that area. Good way how to learn is by imitating successful people. All kids do that because it is in our nature. Kids are learning by watching adults and then by repeating what they see. You just have to find someone who already did what you want to do, find out how he did it and reproduce his actions. Seeing someone as an example makes it easier to repeat the process for you. If he could do it, you can do it too. Being successful is usually not about being extraordinary, but about doing basic and simple things extraordinary well.

Warning! Brain programming and positive thinking

Is brain programming dangerous? If you know what you want, it is not dangerous. How does mind programming work? First you focus on your clear goal. Then you visualize your goal and fill your mind with that visualization. By doing this you push out of your mind what you don't want, because there will be no space left for negative thoughts. Our mind does not understand want or don't want – it just goes after the visualization. "I don't want to be ill" does visualize in your brain as an illness and you will become ill. "I want to be healthy" visualization makes you healthy. "I don't want to be healthy" would probably work too, but I haven't tried that out yet. I will stick to a process which has been tried out and which I know works.

When you have programmed your thoughts, your thoughts influence your words and actions. What you say, out loud or as inner speech, influences your actions too. What you do influences your habits. Your habits finally influence your destiny. If you have the destiny of a rich person, you will become rich sooner or later.

Be careful with your thoughts as they influence your destiny. You will get what you are often thinking about. Even if you don't want it.

Each time, when you have nothing better to do, smile and say '*I am happy, healthy, secure, grateful and I will get **what I want**.*' Replace 'what I want' with what you really want. Best time for this exercise is in the morning when you wake up. And don't forget to smile. Be positive about what you want.

As I stated before, your mind does not recognize what is good or what is bad. Good and bad are relative words. You will get what you focus on even if it has negative impact on you. If you spend your time thinking about 'I do not want to be ill.' you will get eventually ill. The brain does not operate with **do** or **don't**. It just visualizes. It is like computer programming. You give your brain a picture or text and it writes down to your sub-conscious mind. Then it operates based on your simplified instructions.

If you have at least basic knowledge of how to reach what you want, your sub-conscious brain will direct your actions towards that goal. You don't have to know everything on that subject. Of course you will try to find and learn everything on the subject which helps you to reach your ultimate goal. But the basic principles have the biggest impact on reaching the goal. Your sub-conscious mind gives you feelings for the right decision. Focus on what makes the biggest impact and skip the rest. If you will not act, it will not work. But if you have different options and can't decide, then trust your gut.

Learn to program your mind

Emptying your mind is a great autosuggestion technique. It is also called *shutting down your inner speech*. It will help you increase your physical, intellectual and psychic abilities. First you have to define your goal in a positive sentence. It can be a sentence like 'I am strong, healthy, happy and wealthy. I will achieve anything I decide to achieve.' When your goal is defined, you enter the state of empty mind and repeat your goal. Third, you return from empty mind state to natural mind state. Fourth, when it will be necessary, your subconscious mind will run and realize your defined program. It takes some time and some practice to have significant results with this technique. I have read that people use of our physical abilities to only 15% of its full potential. By auto programming yourself you can use 30%, which means doubling your strength and other abilities.

Our life is what our thoughts make our life. If we think about happy things, we will be happy. If we think about our failings, we will fail again for sure. If we think about success, we will reach it. If you think often about your fear, your life will be full of fear. If you think about illness often, you will get ill. Your life is what your thoughts make it.

Your thoughts and words create your destiny. In the beginning there was a word. What we say has very big impact on our life. Programming our subconscious mind is not taught at schools and that's a pity. Our mind is the most important tool that we all have and nobody teaches us how to use it more efficiently.

Our sub-conscious mind operates very simply.

You think of something and your mind directs your actions to get it. If you grieve too much and you do not want to live, you can get a cancer. If you are happy to live, you will be healthy. If you want money and have no bad feelings about them, sub-conscious mind guides your actions to get the money. But if you want money and feel bad about them – for example you think that only by being bad person you can become rich and you don't want to become a bad person, you give your mind chaotic commands. You have to give your mind clear order to get rich without having any doubts that this is what you want.

How to visualize

Easiest way is to have pictures of what you want put to a place where you will see them each morning and each evening before you go to bed. It can be next to your bed or it can be a background desktop picture on your computer. If you can't find appropriate picture, write it down in a positive formulation.

If you will write down 'I do not want to be poor.' you will eventually become poor, because **poor** is the keyword your brain will work with. If you write down '**I am rich, happy and healthy.**' your brain will direct your action to make this image a reality.

For example find a photo where you are smiling and you look healthy. Put to the picture heap of money – what a great visualization. You will see yourself as happy, healthy with lot of money in your brain and your brain will direct your actions to make it real. Humans are able to shape their future by shaping their thoughts and beliefs. If your goal is to love your wife, put picture of you two together smiling. It works. That's why so many people have pictures of their wife and kids with themselves – because they are important for them and they want to see them. Visualization works, try it.

How to focus

1. You have to define what the final result of your task is. It may be fun to do something without having a clear result you want to achieve, but this will not make you richer. It is best if you also have fun at doing the task but reaching the goal should be on your mind as often as

possible.

2. You can focus on your task more easily if you already had some experience with doing the task. The more you practice, the easier it gets to focus.

3. You should have feeling of control over your task and the task must be reachable. Ambitious but reachable. When you don't believe in successful finishing of the task, you will hinder yourself from reaching the goal.

Have a feedback if you are on the right track by having partial goals.

27 Recommended reading / listening / watching sources

- Jim Rohn – The Art of Exceptional Living
- Robert Kiyosaki – Rich Dad, Poor Dad
- Dale Carnegie – How to Win Friends & Influence People
- Dale Carnegie – How to Stop Worrying and Start Living
- Napoleon Hill – Think and Grow Rich
- How to Get Rich – Felix Dennis
- Brian Tracy – Million Dollar Habits
- Jack Canfield – The Success Principles
- T. Harv Eker – Secrets of the Millionaire Mind
- Richard Branson – Business Stripped Bare
- John Adair – The Handbook of Management and Leadership
- Richard Templar – The Rules series
- Michael A. Lechter – Protecting Your #1 Asset
- Blair Singer – Sales dogs
- Alice Schroeder – The Snowball: Warren Buffett and the Business of Life
- Jim Collins – Good to Great
- Jay Abraham – Stealth Marketing
- Ivo Toman – The Power Of Inner Speech
- Timothy Ferriss – The 4-Hour Workweek
- Kacper M. Postawski – Powerful Sleep

- John Gray – Men Are from Mars, Women Are from Venus
- Gary Chapman – Anger: Handling a Powerful Emotion in a Healthy Way
- Kenneth H. Blanchard and Spencer Johnson – The One Minute Manager
- Michael E. Gerber – The E-Myth Revisited
- John Virapen – Side Effects: Death
- YouTube "Fear by Konstantin Komarov"
- Teal Scott on youtube

Thank you again for purchasing this book! I hope it gave you inspiration and tools to become better version of yourself.

It is important for me to get your feedback and hear if it was helpful for you! Please write me your comments at andrew.preshovus@gmail.com

Recommend this book to your friends if you liked it and enemies if you did not.

If you would like to receive notifications about future discounts, new How To e-books for free, subscribe to our newsletter on www.preshovus.com.

www.ingramcontent.com/pod-product-compliance
Lightning Source LLC
Chambersburg PA
CBHW071400170526
45165CB00001B/129